THE SMARTEST
RETIREMENT BOOK
YOU'LL EVER READ

THE SMARTEST RETIREMENT BOOK YOU'LL EVER READ

Daniel R. Solin

A PERIGEE BOOK

A PERIGEE BOOK
Published by the Penguin Group
Penguin Group (USA) Inc.
375 Hudson Street, New York, New York 10014, USA
Penguin Group (Canada), 90 Eglinton Avenue East, Suite 700, Toronto, Ontario M4P 2Y3, Canada
(a division of Pearson Penguin Canada Inc.) • Penguin Books Ltd., 80 Strand, London WC2R 0RL,
England • Penguin Group Ireland, 25 St. Stephen's Green, Dublin 2, Ireland (a division of Penguin
Books Ltd.) • Penguin Group (Australia), 250 Camberwell Road, Camberwell, Victoria 3124,
Australia (a division of Pearson Australia Group Pty. Ltd.) • Penguin Books India Pvt. Ltd.,
11 Community Centre, Panchsheel Park, New Delhi—110 017, India • Penguin Group (NZ),
67 Apollo Drive, Rosedale, North Shore 0632, New Zealand (a division of Pearson New Zealand
Ltd.) • Penguin Books (South Africa) (Pty.) Ltd., 24 Sturdee Avenue, Rosebank, Johannesburg 2196,
South Africa
Penguin Books Ltd., Registered Offices: 80 Strand, London WC2R 0RL, England

While the author has made every effort to provide accurate telephone numbers and Internet addresses
at the time of publication, neither the publisher nor the author assumes any responsibility for errors,
or for changes that occur after publication. Further, the publisher does not have any control over and
does not assume any responsibility for author or third-party websites or their content.

PRINTING HISTORY
Perigee hardcover edition / September 2009
Perigee trade paperback edition / August 2010

Perigee trade paperback ISBN: 978-0-399-53634-2

The Library of Congress has cataloged the Perigee hardcover edition as follows:
Solin, Daniel R.
    The smartest retirement book you'll ever read / Daniel R. Solin.
    p.   cm.
    "A Perigee book."
    Includes bibliographical references and index.
    ISBN 978-0-399-53520-8
    1. Retirement income—United States—Planning.   2. Investments—United States.   3. Finance,
Personal—United States.   4. Older people—United States—Finance, Personal.   I. Title.
    HG179.S55238 2009
    332.024'014—dc22   2009014075

PRINTED IN THE UNITED STATES OF AMERICA
10   9   8   7   6

PUBLISHER'S NOTE: This publication is designed to provide accurate and authoritative information
in regard to the subject matter covered. It is sold with the understanding that the publisher is not engaged
in rendering legal, accounting, or other professional services. If you require legal advice or other expert
assistance, you should seek the services of a competent professional. Continued on page 245.

Most Perigee books are available at special quantity discounts for bulk purchases for sales promo-
tions, premiums, fund-raising, or educational use. Special books, or book excerpts, can also be created to fit specific needs. For details, write: Special Markets, Penguin Group (USA) Inc., 375 Hudson
Street, New York, New York 10014.

To all of my colleagues who continue to fight
the good fight: The tide is turning.

CONTENTS

PART FOUR
Cash Made Simple

PART FIVE
Annuities Made Simple

PART SIX
Mining Your Money

PART SEVEN
Simple Steps to Stretch Your Money

PART EIGHT

Social Security and Pensions: Critical Choices

PART NINE

Is Sixty-Five the New Fifty?

PART TEN

Financial Lifelines for Desperate Times

PART FOURTEEN
Where's the Beef?

INTRODUCTION

The (Tall) Tale of Dr. Ivan Jenner

If you can't explain it simply, you don't understand it well enough.
—Albert Einstein

Ivan Jenner was a German engineer whose fascination with the elevator industry brought him to the United States in 1902.

Dr. Jenner, who held a doctorate in mechanical engineering from the prestigious Universität Karlsruhe, had followed in his family's tradition; his father and grandfather were both engineers.

In school he studied the work of Elisha Graves Otis, the founder of Otis elevators. After graduation, Dr. Jenner accepted a job with Otis and moved to the United States, where the company was based. His first assignment was to plan the design and installation of six vertical hydraulic elevators in the Flatiron Building in New York City.

In 1910, Dr. Jenner left Otis and established himself as an elevator consultant, quickly becoming well known for his expertise in the burgeoning industry.

One day he received a call from the owner of one of New York's largest high-rises. The building manager was inundated with complaints about the long wait for elevators. A number of elevator companies had been approached to study the problem, but the quotes just to do the analysis were prohibitively expensive.

Now tenants were threatening to leave. Could Dr. Jenner assist? There was much at stake.

Dr. Jenner was sure he could solve the problem. He asked for an up-front retainer of $1,000. He offered a full refund if the complaints did not stop.

The building manager agreed: He was ready to do whatever was necessary to appease the tenants. He figured he would be spending much, much more to implement the proposed changes.

Dr. Jenner went to work, studying all aspects of the elevators in the building. The elevators were working perfectly, and their "response efficiency" was state of the art. The solution to the complaints came to Dr. Jenner almost immediately.

"What must I do?" the owner asked.

Dr. Jenner's answer: "Install mirrors next to the elevators on every floor."

The owner followed this suggestion. The complaints stopped.

I made this story up.

But this tale does illustrate some points that are important to retirees and those planning for retirement.

The financial industry and employers have their own agenda.

They are determined to push expensive products down your throat. The fact is that simple, commonsense solutions are often better than complex, costly ones.

Keep this one concept in mind as you start the retirement journey: The advice you receive from many retirement "experts" is distorted, misguided, and, as often as not, self-serving.

The goal of this book is to give you the tools you'll need to identify and easily resolve the issues you will confront in retirement, from investing to estate planning.

My recommended solutions are no more complicated than Dr. Jenner's.

Author's Note

I am not affiliated with any of the fund families in the recommended portfolios in this book. I recommend funds managed by Dimensional Fund Advisors to my investment advisory clients but receive no compensation from that firm for doing so.

PART ONE

Rethink Retirement Investing

How you invest *during* retirement is as critical as how you invest in preparing for retirement. Things are never as simple and automatic as they once may have been—you worked hard, saved, and then sat back and collected your benefits. You can't rely on someone else coming up with the cash you'll need once you stop working.

CHAPTER 1

Deflating Inflation

Inflation is when you pay fifteen dollars for the ten-dollar
haircut you used to get for five dollars when you had hair.
—Sam Ewing, humorist

Retirees should be as concerned about investing their retirement nest eggs as they are about withdrawing from them—the 2008 market crash exacerbated these concerns and makes this issue even more critical.

Fortunately, Smart Investing before or during retirement is not difficult. While you'll hear lots of ballyhoo about the special investment needs of retirees, the basic investment rules—the Smart Investing rules—are the same for everyone, no matter what their age or stage of their investing lives.

In Chapter 5 and Appendix B, I provide recommended portfolios that will take the mystery out of this process. Before jumping in, we'll review in the chapters ahead some basic investing principles you need to understand.

Let's start with the most commonly overlooked one: inflation.

Inflation: The Natural Predator of Your Nest Egg

Retirees understandably worry about the stock market's gyrations. Who wouldn't, especially given the current unprecedented financial meltdown? But they don't spend nearly as much time fretting about inflation.

In recent years, inflation doesn't seem to have been much of an issue. For more than a decade, the nation's annual inflation rate has rarely inched above 3 percent. As 2009 began, economists were far more worried about deflation.

Yet even a seemingly innocuous inflation rate can flatten the cushion of a retiree's otherwise solid budget. When inflation is running at 3 percent, the value of $100 will plummet to $76 in just ten years. If you wait two decades, the value of that $100 is worth no more than $56.

It's easy to illustrate how destructive inflation can be if you look at hypothetical portfolios of retirees from twenty or thirty years ago. Today's retirees can easily live that long or longer.

I used the inflation calculator from the federal Bureau of Labor Statistics to see how much money a retiree would need today to match the buying power of an American who retired with a $500,000 nest egg twenty years ago. Thanks to inflation, today's retiree would require $924,695. (You can play with your own numbers at www.bls .gov/data/inflation_calculator.htm.)

The current crop of retirees will likely feel the pinch of inflation more acutely because it is likely they will have to spend more on medical costs, which have been rising faster than inflation.

Unfortunately, the only inflation indexing that most retirees can count on today is their Social Security checks, which provide an annual cost of living allowance.

Countless research has illustrated that conservative portfolios run the risk of running on fumes. One landmark study examined what would happen if an investor withdrew 6 percent a year from an all-bond portfolio. The study concluded that the investor had only a 27 percent chance of having anything left after thirty years.

As you contemplate how you're going to structure your portfolio in retirement, you'll want to plan to deal with inflation.

The solution—as hard as this might be to swallow in today's vola-tile markets—involves adding stocks to your portfolio. I'll discuss exactly how you should do that in Part Two.

What's the Point?

If you don't fortify your portfolio against inflation, you're likely to outlive your money.

CHAPTER 2

When Conservative Is Risky

The myth of the income portfolio is among the most
damaging myths foisted on the public.
—Harold Evensky, investment advisor and author of
Retirement Income Redesigned: Master Plans for Distribution

Imagine a Thanksgiving feast that ends with pumpkin pie. After all
the guests have eaten, only a few crumbs remain. Too bad for the
hosts who were counting on leftovers.

A disappearing pie is an apt analogy to describe the income-only
approach to investing, a wildly popular strategy with many retirees,
who believe that they will never run out of money as long as they don't
touch their principal. They build financial bomb shelters with a collection of bonds, certificates of deposit, savings accounts, and anything
else that doesn't seem to carry any risk.

Many retirees fear that they won't live long enough to survive
a nasty market downturn—especially without paychecks coming
in—so they believe the best solution is to avoid anything that smacks
of volatility—like stocks.

This approach often fails because it provides the interest and
income—but that won't be enough to keep up with inflation. (See
Chapter 1 if you need reminding about the insidious aspects of
inflation.)

If you focus exclusively on income and banish stocks from your portfolio, you won't see the long-term growth your portfolio needs. It's been ages since stocks generated meaningful dividends, so there's little place at the income-only table for them.

Without stocks, retirement accounts inevitably lose ground to inflation—and a retiree's purchasing power will erode dramatically. Eventually, all that's left to consume is the principal and, eventually, the crumbs.

To keep that from happening, you'll need to add a globally diversified portfolio of stocks to your portfolio. Keep reading. You'll learn the right and wrong ways to do just that.

What's the Point?

Investing in an income-only portfolio can be risky.

CHAPTER 3

Stocks for the Timid

If you know the grocery money is set aside and how the bills will
be paid in the next couple of years, you have staying power to
stick with your investment portfolio in very tough markets.
—Lane Jones, principal, Evensky & Katz, investment advisory firm

These days, it takes a lot of courage to invest in stocks. Even though you may be convinced it makes sense to do so, you're worried about having to sell in a down market.

Think about it this way: You'll invest for growth through a balance of stocks and fixed-income investments. You'll make yearly withdrawals from your entire portfolio—a certain percentage from your overall holdings—rather than simply scooping up any interest and income.

You'll harvest the low-hanging fruit first, like stock dividends and income from treasuries or other bonds. This allows you to avoid transaction fees and taxes for selling off assets.

After the easy money is gone, you might need to liquidate some stocks as well.

This "total return" approach doesn't require you to invest without a seat belt. During turbulent times, you'll need a cash cushion.

In retirement, you should set aside enough of a cash reserve to provide for your living expenses for *at least* two years.

So how would this work? Let's say you have committed to a

portfolio of 60 percent stocks and 40 percent bonds (which may be too aggressive for many retirees). When you add a 10 percent cash allocation, the percentage of your stock and bond holdings in your total portfolio would drop to 55 percent and 35 percent, respectively.

You can keep that cash in a short term, FDIC-insured savings account or a money market account with a major fund family like Vanguard, Fidelity, or Charles Schwab.

Every month you'd write a check from one of these accounts and deposit the cash into your checking account. In a sense, you're generating a monthly paycheck.

Then it won't be as worrisome when the S&P 500 Index, or any other market benchmark, is experiencing a decline.

Once your cash dips below the one-year level, you'll replenish the account by selling some of your holdings. But what if stocks are getting pummeled during that period?

As an interim measure, don't touch the stocks. Instead, draw down your bond holdings—which should be composed of high-quality short- and intermediate-term bonds. The bond funds in my recommended portfolios fit into these categories. (You can find my recommended portfolios in Chapter 5 and Appendix B.)

Don't forget to rebalance your holdings periodically. You want to keep your basic asset allocation intact. By *asset allocation* I am referring to the division of your investment portfolio between stocks and bonds.

Ultimately this should give you at least several years before you'd have to touch any stocks. This strategy makes it unlikely that you would have to sell equities at fire-sale prices during a bear market.

What's the Point?

A two-year cash cushion and a well-balanced portfolio can help reduce your portfolio's volatility and give you the courage to Invest In stocks.

PART TWO

Stocks Made Simple

Stocks permit you to keep pace with inflation. In the following chapters, I discuss exactly how you should select stocks for your retirement portfolio.

CHAPTER 4

Stock-Picking Perils

Most people get interested in stocks when everyone
else is. The time to get interested is when no one
else is. You can't buy what is popular and do well.
—Warren Buffett, billionaire investor

Your investments should be divided into stocks and bonds. While there are plenty of misconceptions about bonds (which I deal with in Part Three), it is stocks that cause the most anxiety.

In this part, I discuss basic principles to guide you in making decisions concerning the stock portion of your investment portfolio.

A *Wall Street Journal* article that ran during 2008's tumultuous market free fall stated the obvious: "There are now probably no widow and orphan stocks on Wall Street."

The journalist was referring to blue chip stocks that used to kick out dependable dividends and provide steady, if slow, price appreciation. Over the years, plenty of retirees gravitated to these kinds of stocks. They seemed like the "safest" stocks available.

But look at what's happened to some of those safe stocks lately.

Along with a dramatic drop in the overall stock market, shareholders in some individual stocks have been hit particularly hard. You need to look no further than the entire U.S. auto and financial services industries for particularly gripping examples.

Despite the misery that the decline of these and other blue chip stocks has unleashed, it's a positive development that people now acknowledge that the strategy of stock picking—even when you think you're working with safe stocks—is a bust. Frankly, the strategy never made sense.

There's been a long history in this country of previously solid stocks disappointing shareholders. The most important take-away lesson for every investor is this: Investing in *any* individual stock is never going to be a judicious move.

The potential gains for any individual stock can't make up for the tremendous risk of holding it.

Does this mean you should boycott stocks? Absolutely not. What retirees and investors of any age should do is embrace stocks as an entire asset class. You want to own stocks in a bundle. Owning a broadly diversified bucket of domestic and international stocks is far less risky than owning individual stocks.

Many retirees worry about the inherent volatility of stocks, but when you look at fairly modest time horizons, the risk doesn't look so bad.

While I would never suggest that your portfolio comprise *only* stocks, during the past fifty years the worst four-year annualized loss for an all-stock portfolio was less than 2 percent. If you look at any ten-year rolling period during the past five decades through December 2008, a globally diversified, all-stock portfolio registered profits 99.1 percent of the time.

It's certainly something to think about.

What's the Point?

Investing in individual stocks is too risky for most investors.
There are no safe individual stocks.

CHAPTER 5

Balancing Risk and Returns

Take calculated risks. That is quite different from being rash.
—George S. Patton

Most retirees would love a portfolio that offers big rewards with little risk—but that's never going to happen. In the investing world, risk and reward are kissing cousins.

The U.S. Treasury Department doesn't have to lure investors with a high return for its risk-free bills because people aren't afraid of investing in them. Because the ups and downs of stocks are far more uncertain, the financial enticements have to be greater to attract takers.

Performance statistics bear this out. Going back to the 1920s, the riskiest investments have generated the highest average annual returns:

Small-cap stocks	12.5%
Large-cap stocks	10.4%
Long-term government bonds	5.4%
Treasury bills (cash)	3.7%

The goal of any investor, and certainly any retiree, is to perform a balancing act. A model portfolio will contain both low-risk/low-return and high-risk/high-return investments. Like Goldilocks's perfect porridge, you want a portfolio that's not too hot and not too cold.

The typical retiree should have a healthy dose of stocks in the mix. Anywhere from 40 to 50 percent stocks for a new retiree is often recommended.

Here's a model portfolio to consider. This one consists of funds managed by Vanguard. Comparable funds are available from other fund families. (In Appendix B, I give the historical risk and return data for each of these portfolios. Appendix A consists of the Asset Allocation Questionnaire to help you determine which portfolio is right for you.)

If you decide to open an account with Vanguard, for instance, the stock and bond portions of your portfolio would appear as follows:

- 70 percent of your stock allocation in the Vanguard Total Stock Market Index Fund (VTSMX)

- 30 percent of your stock allocation in the Vanguard Total International Stock Index Fund (VGTSX)

- 100 percent of your bond allocation in the Vanguard Total Bond Market Index Fund (VBMFX)

You'll note that all the portfolios I recommend consist solely of globally diversified, low-cost index funds. By *index fund*, I mean a fund that holds all of the stocks in a specific segment of the market. For example, an S&P 500 index fund holds the stocks of the 500 widely held companies that make up that index. In this way, without trying to time the market or pick stock winners, this type of fund will always match the returns of the stocks of those five hundred companies, minus the low costs incurred by the fund.

The accompanying chart tells you exactly how to invest your money, depending on which level of risk is appropriate for you. I have used Vanguard funds as an example. In Appendix B, I set forth similar portfolios from other fund families. I also provide long-term risk and return data.

COMPOSITION OF FOUR VANGUARD MODEL PORTFOLIOS

Fund Name	Low Risk	Medium-Low Risk	Medium-High Risk	High Risk
Total Stock Market Index Fund (VTSMX)	14%	28%	42%	56%
Total International Stock Index Fund (VGTSX)	6%	12%	18%	24%
Total Bond Market Index Fund (VBMFX)	80%	60%	40%	20%
Total assets	100%	100%	100%	100%

Investing in low-cost index funds for the stock and bond portions of your portfolio is the most intelligent way to invest. In the next chapter, I'll tell you why.

What's the Point?

Your portfolio should have a healthy mix of low-risk/low-return and high-risk/high-return investments.

CHAPTER 6

High Fund Expenses Are Your Mortal Enemy

The deadliest sin of all is the high cost of owning some mutual funds. What might seem to be low fees, expressed in tenths of 1 percent, can easily cost an investor tens of thousands of dollars over a lifetime.
—Arthur Levitt, former chairman of the U.S. Securities and Exchange Commission

To invest successfully in retirement, you need to give your portfolio a checkup: High fees can seriously jeopardize its health. They are your mortal enemy.

When you use inexpensive index funds in your retirement portfolio, you minimize fund fees while maximizing your returns. Show me a portfolio dominated by low-cost index funds, and it's extremely likely I'll find an owner who fared better financially—over the long run—than investors using more expensive, actively managed funds (for which the fund manager is trying to outperform a given benchmark).

Since the 1960s, academics and other researchers have been cranking out study after study proving that simple index funds produce superior track records over the long haul.

Despite the avalanche of research supporting indexing superiority, these funds aren't popular with individual investors.

Why not? Brokers view index funds as a threat to *their* wealth. Index funds don't generate fat commissions, so you can't expect any enthusiasm from them about indexing.

Here's one more reason why indexing remains a relative wallflower. Most investors don't understand how fees can erode a portfolio.

While retirees are well aware of the debilitating effect of inflation on the cost of a pound of hamburger, few investors understand the internal costs of the funds in their portfolio.

You'll learn more about why indexing is a retiree's best friend in the next chapter.

What's the Point?

Indexing is the superior way to invest.

CHAPTER 7

The Investing Secret Your Broker Won't Tell You

Index funds have a large following among institutional investors
such as pension funds and insurance companies. Ironically,
one of the most vocal advocates of index funds for
individual investors is Warren Buffett, self-made billionaire
and chairman of Berkshire Hathaway Inc. [who] made
his fortune through individual stock selection.
—Richard A. Ferri, CFA, author of *All About Asset Allocation*

ndexing can make you feel like an investing genius.
Here are the major benefits of indexing:

- Market returns (which are superior returns)

- Low cost

- Broad diversification

- Tax efficiency

- Minimal cash holdings

Let's take a look at these more closely.

Market Returns

Index funds make a simple promise: Everybody who indexes will earn market returns minus low transaction costs.

Here's an example: If the S&P 500 index (the popular benchmark for blue chip stocks) generated a yearly return of 9 percent, you could count on the Vanguard 500 Index Fund, the Fidelity Spartan 500 Index Fund, or some other large-cap index fund to produce a return that's almost identical.

The goal of an index fund manager is to be a clone of a corresponding index.

When an index stumbles, so will its index fund. When the index is doing well, so will the index fund. Over time, stocks and bonds of every size and category have grown, which means index funds have too.

It is perfectly understandable if you're not impressed by "average" market returns. After all, it's far easier to tout the stellar returns of carefully selected actively managed funds. Unfortunately, these returns are almost always ephemeral. An actively managed fund can enjoy a streak of phenomenal luck—but nearly all actively managed funds eventually stumble. Their long-term (and even shorter-term) performance returns lag behind comparable index funds.

Why do proponents of actively managed funds struggle so much against those average returns?

These stock jockeys eventually smack into a brick wall called the "efficient market." Think about it this way: Wall Street is transparent—any news about any stock quickly makes the rounds, and the stock is adjusted accordingly. Consequently, it's almost impossible for professionals to outsmart all the other investors trying to beat the markets.

The difficulty of surpassing index returns on a sustained basis is even harder than it appears, thanks to something called "survivor bias." Every year, a huge number of actively managed funds go out of business. During one recent five-year period, according to Standard

& Poor's, more than one in four stock funds vanished. The funds that disappear are typically the ones with terrible performance statistics. Fund companies will often get rid of the embarrassing funds by merging them into more successful ones.

With the dead bodies hidden away, the remaining actively managed funds look better than they deserve.

Low Cost and Lovin' It

Index funds are the cheapest game in town. The Vanguard 500 Index Fund, which is the nation's most popular index fund, charges shareholders just 0.15 percent to manage their assets. That means if you had $10,000 invested in the fund, your tab for the year would be a paltry $15. There are even cheaper class shares for larger investors. For a new shareholder who invests at least $100,000 in the Vanguard 500 Index, the cost would drop to 0.07 percent, or only $70 a year.

The typical mutual fund can easily charge ten times more than a comparable index fund. People don't appreciate that price gap, because the difference doesn't seem wide. A fund that charges 1.7 percent doesn't seem like a porker compared to one that charges 0.07 percent. In reality, the gulf is huge.

Let's suppose you invested $50,000 in a stock index fund that charges 0.20 percent in expenses, and your neighbor invested the same amount in an actively managed stock fund that charges 2 percent. Let's assume you both earned an annual 8 percent return before expenses.

A decade later, your index fund would be worth $105,964. The fund of the poor guy next door would be worth $89,542. Your neighbor's cost for holding this fund would have been $16,422.

Broad Diversification

Index funds hold more securities than actively managed funds. By diversifying the number of holdings, index funds reduce the risk of having a concentrated position in a smaller number of stocks.

Tax Efficiency

When judging mutual funds, investors look at total returns. But performance statistics can be misleading. When investments aren't sheltered in retirement accounts, *after-tax* returns are the key feature.

Taxes can mangle the returns of actively managed funds. Too many portfolio managers trade stocks with little regard for the tax consequences that are borne by the investor. Index funds are considered paragons of tax efficiency because there is little turnover in their portfolios.

John Bogle, the former head of the Vanguard Group, conducted a study that illustrated how devastating the tax bite can be for actively managed funds. Over a sixteen-year period, Bogle concluded that investors kept only 47 percent of the cumulative return of the average actively managed stock fund. Indexers kept 87 percent.

Can you afford to leave that much of your money on the table?

Minimal Cash Holdings

Large cash holdings reduce returns in a rising market. Index funds typically have less cash holdings than actively managed funds because they don't have to keep cash on hand to time the market. Index fund portfolios stay focused on meeting the returns of the index.

What's the Point?

Investors who index achieve *superior* returns.

CHAPTER 8

Make a Date with Target-Date Funds

There's plenty of appeal behind target-retirement funds,
also known variously as target-date or target-maturity
funds, primarily because they are so easy to use.
—Christopher Davis, Morningstar analyst

Target-date funds can be used by investors both before and during
retirement.

These funds rebalance the percentage of bonds versus stocks
in the fund as the target date of the funds gets closer.

Target-date funds were designed for those who'd like someone
else to do the heavy lifting. They're also known as target-maturity,
life-cycle, or target-retirement funds, and they're promoted for retirees, young adults in their first jobs . . . and every other demographic
group in between.

Mutual fund companies aren't the only ones enthused about
target-date funds. Not long ago, Congress lent its seal of approval by
sanctioning their widespread use in 401(k) lineups.

There's nothing magical about target-date funds. They can be a wel-
come tool for anyone who thinks that investing is tedious or beyond

comprehension. (But even target-date funds require that you at least skim through the owner's manual.)

You and your target-date fund are supposed to grow old together: As you age, your fund slowly turns gray by growing more conservative as you head toward retirement.

The fund's manager takes care of the underlying investing mechanics. You just need to select a fund that closely matches the rough date of your anticipated retirement. If you're planning on retiring in 2011, you could choose the Vanguard Target Retirement 2010 fund, or even the Vanguard Target Retirement 2015 fund.

A target-date fund serves as an umbrella, which contains a collection of underlying mutual funds or exchange-traded funds that invest in a variety of assets: blue chips and small caps, foreign stocks, and bonds. As the years go by, bonds shove some of the stocks out of the portfolio, making it more conservative.

For example, the Vanguard Target Retirement 2015 fund held 37.3 percent in bonds recently, whereas the bond exposure was 46.3 percent for the more conservative Vanguard Target Retirement 2010 fund.

Thanks to action by Congress, target-date funds have become more popular as 401(k) investment choices. Employers are now more likely to use these autopilot funds as default choices when workers don't check off an investment choice. Congress also gave the workplace a green light to use target-date funds when they automatically enroll employees in 401(k) plans.

If you're invested in a target-based fund at your workplace, you may be inclined to keep it when you retire. Before you do that or hunt for a new one, make sure it fits your needs.

There are roughly three hundred target-date funds—and the number is growing. Plenty of them are dogs. You won't necessarily know that by looking at performance figures because quite a few of them didn't even exist three years ago. Focus on costs instead: According to a recent study, the annual expense ratio for target-date funds ranged from 0.21 percent up to 1.4 percent.

Choose the cheapest target-date fund. Your best bet is to stick with funds for which the underlying choices are low-cost index funds, like the Vanguard Target Retirement funds. They offer the lowest price tags.

High expenses can silently chew up your returns and your account balance, especially when compounded over time. Because the fees are sucked out automatically, investors typically never notice. That's exactly what fund companies are counting on.

Beyond price, examine how target-date funds spread around their assets. On this issue, these funds are all over the board. A study conducted by Target Date Analytics examined target-date funds marketed to investors retiring in 2010 and determined that the stock allocation ranged from 20 to 70 percent. That's a huge range!

The three dominant players in the target-date field—Vanguard, Fidelity, and T. Rowe Price—all offer retirees a good dose of stocks in their most conservative offerings.

There's no need to bail from a fund after it reaches its target date; it will just continue to grow more conservative. Vanguard Target Retirement 2005 recently had 58 percent of its investment in bonds and the rest in stocks. In a few years, the fund will eventually arrive at a 70/30 split of bonds and stocks.

What's the Point?

Target-date retirement funds can serve a dual purpose:
They can help you reach your retirement goals, and they
can be excellent investments during retirement.

CHAPTER 9

Resist the Allure
of ETFs

The explosive asset growth in exchange-traded funds
over the past few years is testament to the investment
edge ETFs can add to an investment portfolio.
—IndexUniverse.com

There's another route to capture market returns: indexing through Exchange Traded Funds (ETFs).

ETFs used to be an oddity. Today they're one of the fastest-growing investment products in the world. In 1993, a solitary Exchange Traded Fund existed. It took two years before another one surfaced. But fifteen years later, according to the Investment Company Institute, the number of ETFs has soared to 697. Plenty of industry insiders don't expect that momentum to stall.

Why all the fuss? ETFs look a lot like index mutual funds, but they are devoted to many more investing niches.

Each ETF tracks its matching index—and there are many indexes used as benchmarks. The ETF's collection of underlying stocks or bonds is expected to track its designated index as closely as possible. In fact, most ETFs must maintain a 99 percent correlation to their benchmark.

What makes ETFs different is that they're traded like stocks. To buy or sell ETF shares, you must place an order through a brokerage firm, just as you would if you wanted to buy shares of any individual stock.

So, what role should ETFs play in your retirement portfolio? The answer might surprise you: None.

At present, most ETFs are not less expensive than the low-cost index funds in my recommended portfolios. In addition, the commissions you incur on ETF purchases will reduce your returns—especially if you buy regularly over an extended period of time. With index funds, you buy directly from the fund family—like Vanguard or Fidelity—without paying any commissions.

Beyond a commission, you'll also have to pay a bit extra when you buy shares in an ETF, thanks to something called the "bid-ask spread." This spread refers to the gap between the market price for buying the ETF versus selling the investment. For example, if the bid price is $40 and the ask price is $41.50, the bid-ask spread is $1.50. As a purchaser, you will pay the ask price. The seller receives the bid price. Securities dealers pocket the difference. Because mutual funds aren't traded as stocks, mutual funds don't have bid–ask spreads.

ETFs are also less convenient. If you are investing in index funds, you can choose to automatically invest dividends back into the fund. ETFs pay distributions in cash that would likely end up in your brokerage firm account. You'd then have to figure out how to invest the cash.

Some of the much-touted benefits of ETFs are actually a curse. As ETFs gained in popularity, new entrants had to find a different way to distinguish themselves. Big players like Barclays and State Street Global Advisors already had the broadly diversified ETFs covered, so other fund managers aimed for all kinds of oddball niches.

No one needs an ETF that invests in a bunch of cancer research stocks or a bundle of stocks that links its fortunes to maritime shippers. The availability of all of these ETF sectors tempts investors to place risky bets they should avoid.

What's the Point?

Most investors do not need ETFs in their retirement portfolios.

PART THREE

Bonds Made Simple

Bonds are a critical part of your retirement portfolio but not the holy grail that many people think when they are looking for a safe and conservative investment. In this part, I demystify the process of making the right bond choices.

CHAPTER 10

Bonds in a Nutshell

A fixed-income instrument plays three primary roles in a
portfolio: to serve as a liquid reserve in the event of emergencies;
to generate a stable cash flow; and to provide the portfolio
with stability, allowing investors to take equity risk.
—Larry Swedroe, CPA, author of *The Only Guide to Alternative
Investments You'll Ever Need*

Most investors should own bonds. They're even more critical for retirees. A firm foundation with bonds will give you the confidence to include more stocks—the growth vehicle—in your portfolio.

Because there are a lot of bond options out there, you need to understand some basics and read some scary stories. The goal of this part of the book is to demystify the process of selecting bonds for your investment portfolio. Fortunately, this is a lot easier than you might think.

Use Bonds for the Right Reasons

Resist any temptation to make a killing by trying to guess interest rate movements or chase unusually high yields.

Use bonds to generate a steady income in retirement and to reduce the risk of your portfolio. When a portfolio's fixed-income foundation is fortified against financial earthquakes, investors can feel more confident about taking risks with stocks. You'll use stocks to supply a portfolio's octane and bonds to provide the stable foundation.

Stocks—not bonds—are the proper asset for taking risks.

You can also use the safest bonds, including money markets, to stash cash that you can't afford to lose. For instance, U.S. Treasury bonds are the nation's safest bonds; the entire government would have to go bankrupt before they would default.

Avoid Greed

American investors commonly sabotage their stock portfolios by chasing hot stock returns. When financial talking heads start raving about a mutual fund or stock that's generating eye-popping returns, investors rush to buy it. Of course, the overheated returns come with a price: vastly increased risk.

The same phenomenon occurs with bonds. Plenty of conservative fixed-income investors fall in love with speculative bonds for their outsize yields, but they ignore their sizable risk.

Compare Similar Bonds

Often the bonds providing the most alluring returns are generated by portfolio managers who expose their clients to extra risk. For instance, when one intermediate-term bond fund is offering a 7 percent yield and the competition is offering 3 percent, the manager with the better yield isn't necessarily superior; he's likely playing with fire. While others might be heavily invested in U.S. Treasuries and other safe bonds, he's juicing his returns with dicier bonds, like emerging market debt or junk bonds.

Even managers of staid short-term bond funds have been caught trying to juice their returns. (You'll see some disastrous examples in Chapter 11.)

Ignore Individual Corporate Bonds

That's right—you don't need individual corporate bonds. You have to look only at the Wall Street carnage that began in 2008 to see why individual corporate bonds are too hot to handle.

The problem with blue chip corporate debt is hardly a recent phenomenon. In the spring of 2002, telecom giant WorldCom had an excellent bond rating; within a few weeks, the rating had dropped into junk bond status, and WorldCom declared bankruptcy.

Beyond the scary anecdotes, investment-grade and high-yield corporate debt share a troubling characteristic: Corporate bonds tend to flounder during the same periods as equities—and when stocks have tanked, you want bonds to step up and serve as the life raft.

Your bond investments should be limited to low-cost bond index funds that track the performance of a broad, market-weighted bond index. The bond funds in my recommended portfolios meet these criteria. They are highly diversified, with minimal exposure to corporate debt.

Diversify the Risk

Except for U.S. Treasuries, you're tempting fate if you invest in individual bonds. Retirees can safely invest in Treasuries because they are backed by the full faith and credit of the U.S. government. Other types of issuers, even those with seemingly impeccable fiscal track records, pose a credit danger. If you hold a few municipal bonds (tax-free bonds issued by city and local governments), for instance, you face the risk of one or two of them blowing up and gutting your portfolio.

If you think municipal bonds never default, think again. In 1991, more than $5 billion in municipal bonds defaulted. In 2008, notable municipal bond defaults included a $3.8 billion sewer bond default by Jefferson County, Alabama, and a Chapter 9 bankruptcy filing by the town of Vallejo, California, involving $280 million in bonds.

Diversification shrinks risk. The best way to diversify is to invest in bonds through a low-cost bond index fund, which may own hundreds of different issues.

Many bond funds have yearly expense ratios in the 1 percent range. That's way too high. My recommended Vanguard Total Bond Market Index Fund has an expense ratio of only 0.19 percent.

Morningstar (www.morningstar.com) is an excellent resource for investors wondering about the quality of the bonds in a particular mutual fund. Just call up a fund's profile and click on "Portfolio." You can also find this information in a fund's annual report.

What's the Point?

Most investors should invest in a broadly diversified,
low-cost, bond index fund.

CHAPTER 11

Blindsided by Bonds

The safe way to double your money is to fold it
over once and put it in your pocket.
—Kin Hubbard, American humorist

When the housing market began imploding in 2007, some retirees—including those who hadn't bought or sold a house in decades—became unwitting victims.

These conservative investors got sideswiped by the mortgage fiasco simply because they thought they could safely earn a little more yield on what was supposed to be a nearly risk-free investment: ultra-short bond funds.

They hardly seemed like daredevils when they plunked their money into these funds that invested in fixed-income securities with extremely short maturities—rather than the even-tamer certificates of deposit (CDs), money markets, Treasury bills, and other types of bond funds.

Ultra-short bond funds, which don't assume much interest rate or credit risk, have traditionally been able to generate slightly more return, without posing much risk to principal.

What investors didn't anticipate was the eagerness of some ultra-short bond fund managers to generate fatter returns by loading up on securities that depended on the health of the housing market.

Some of these funds eventually tanked.

What was most startling about this fiasco was who the guilty parties were. Among the most battered funds were those managed by a few of the financial industry's most respected players: Charles Schwab, Fidelity, and State Street. Their corporate names were plastered on funds that ended 2007 in negative territory and continued to crater in 2008.

Shareholders in these nightmare funds fled. Lawyers began filing lawsuits and seeking arbitration hearings against the corporate sponsors.

I share this cautionary tale because it illustrates what can occasionally go wrong when retirees are searching for safe places to park their money.

The only "risk-free" investments are FDIC-insured CDs and Treasury bills, notes, and bonds. (There are even rumblings about the safety of those investments, given the current economic climate.) All other investments have risk. There is no additional return without increased risk.

What's the Point?

Risk is the foundation of all returns. There is no free lunch.
This applies to bonds as well as stocks.

CHAPTER 12

Avoid Treasury Inflation-Protected Securities

Since TIPS are inflation indexed and government guaranteed,
they are as close to a riskless investment as I can conceive.
—John Brynjolfsson, managing director and
portfolio manager, PIMCO

No doubt about it: Treasury Inflation-Protected Securities (TIPS)
represent an excellent hedge against inflation.

TIPS were unveiled in 1997 by the U.S. Treasury Department.
Today they represent about 10 percent of the Treasury stockpile.

TIPS differ from traditional Treasuries because they're designed
to provide a guaranteed "real" rate of return. This is the return after
inflation erodes an investment. Regular bonds don't provide inflation
protection.

Here's how the inflation protection works: TIPS are widely extolled
for behaving as a separate asset class. This means TIPS possess a very
low correlation with stocks—even less so than traditional types of
bonds. What's more, just like other Treasuries, TIPS are exempt from
state and local taxes.

What do I have against TIPS, and why aren't they included in my recommended portfolios? Here are my three reasons:

- **Lower returns:** The returns generated by TIPS are lower than non-inflation-protected bonds. This makes sense. You are paying for the inflation protection.

- **Volatility:** Take a look at the data in the accompanying chart, which was current as of November 30, 2008. The chart compares the one-, three-, and five-year returns of Vanguard's Total Bond Market Index Fund, which is not inflation protected, to Vanguard's Inflation-Protected Securities Fund. Note the combination of greater volatility and lower returns for the inflation-protected fund.

Fund name	1 Year	3 Year	5 Year
Vanguard Total Bond Market Index Fund (VBMFX)	1.89%	4.61%	4.07%
Vanguard Inflation-Protected Securities Fund (VIPSX)	−7.82%	1.51%	3.01%

- **Deflation:** Deflation is the opposite of inflation. During deflationary periods, there is a decrease in the price level of goods and services. The extra cost of TIPS gets you nothing during periods of deflation.

If you are not persuaded and want to add TIPS to your portfolio, you can buy them directly at auction through Treasury Direct (800-722-2678 or www.treasurydirect.gov), but the auctions are infrequent.

You can purchase individual TIPS through a brokerage firm. You'll want to be careful about costs. Get quotes from two or three firms. You can buy TIPS through index funds or Exchange Traded Funds. The two funds I recommend are Vanguard Inflation-Protected Securities Fund (VIPSX) and iShares Barclays TIPS Bond Fund (TIP).

It's best to hold TIPS inside a retirement account because they're tax hogs. TIPS investors pay yearly federal income taxes on any increases in principal, even though they won't pocket that money until they sell the bond or it matures.

What's the Point?

Most investors do not need TIPS in their portfolios.

PART FOUR

Cash Made Simple

Cash management can add value to your retirement portfolio. In this section, I show you how to increase the returns on the cash portion of your investment holdings without increasing risk.

CHAPTER 13

You Need Cash Insurance

Bank failures are caused by depositors who don't deposit
enough money to cover losses due to mismanagement.
—Dan Quayle, former vice president

Now that we have discussed the glamorous topics of stocks and bonds, let's talk about cash. You have a number of options for investing your cash, none of which involve stuffing it under the mattress. The purpose of this part of the book is to be sure you select the option that is right for you.

There's nothing like a highly publicized bank run to panic customers—and make that mattress look pretty appealing.

During the summer of 2008, consumer interest in the Federal Deposit Insurance Corp. soared when three banks failed within three weeks. According to a report in the *Baltimore Sun*, the FDIC's website was swamped with nine million hits a day after IndyMac Bank in Southern California, the most heavily publicized failure, collapsed.

Bank failures are frightening. It's a riveting media story when hundreds of bank customers stand in line for hours to pull out their cash. Yet the reality is that bank collapses have remained rare, even as the credit crisis gripped the country and led to unfathomable bailouts of some of the biggest financial institutions. Near the tail end of 2008, just 2 percent of the roughly eight-five hundred banks and savings institutions had made it on to the FDIC's "problem list."

Ironically, the nation's credit collapse made it easier to avoid becoming a victim of a banking collapse. Here's what you need to know to stay safe.

Watch the Bank Insurance Ceiling

The FDIC used to insure the cash in your bank account (or spread out in many accounts within one bank) up to $100,000, but until January 1, 2010, the federal government will raise the cash ceiling to $250,000 per depositor. (The ceiling is already that high for retirement accounts, such as individual retirement accounts.)

Consult EDIE

The FDIC's site has a wonderful tool—EDIE the Estimator—that will add up all of your accounts and alert you if you're in danger of exceeding the limits at any FDIC-insured bank. To use EDIE (www2.fdic.gov/edie/index.html), you'll need a list of your deposit accounts at FDIC-insured banks, the current balances, and the names of all account owners and beneficiaries.

Divide Up the Cash

If you don't let your bank deposits exceed the limits, you're safe. One obvious way to do that is to spread your accounts around to different financial institutions and then monitor them to make sure the cash doesn't creep past the limits. You may have to move cash when banks merge.

Consider Using a Registry

Admittedly, some investors will consider scattering money among different banks a hassle. If you're in that camp, you may be interested in something called the Certificate of Deposit Account Registry Service (CDARS; www.cdars.com).

CDARS allows you to select one bank in its network and then choose a CD of various maturities from that one institution. You can then invest any sum of money in that CD and not worry about exceeding the FDIC limits.

Why? Because the service, which represents more than two thousand banks, divides large investments into deposits below the ceiling and places them at different banks. The customer gets the same rate as that offered by the selected institution, and he or she will have to deal with only one statement.

CDARS was created because small banks were always grumbling that they couldn't compete with the big boys like Bank of America or Wells Fargo. Even though smaller banks can offer higher rates, many customers mistakenly believe that giant banks are safer (the assumption being that regulators won't let the Goliaths collapse). The network was considered an attempt to level the playing field.

Before embracing this strategy, compare CD rates outside this network; you might find more competitive rates elsewhere.

Know What's Covered

The FDIC will protect all sorts of bank investments, including CDs, savings accounts, and checking accounts.

The protection doesn't extend to the contents of safe deposit boxes. The insurance also doesn't cover such investments as stocks, annuities, and life insurance. The bank may sell you one hundred shares of Home Depot stock, but it can't guarantee what happens to it after you buy it.

What's the Point?

Make sure that your bank and credit union deposits don't exceed the FDIC's insurance limits.

CHAPTER 14

The Holy Grail

More Reward, Same Risk

A lot of people who are in cash are more interested
in return of principal than return on principal, so they
don't care about the yield, and that shows.
—Peter Crane, *Money Fund Intelligence* newsletter

When people look for a place to park their cash, they often end up at the local branch of a well-known bank—one that's a two- or three-minute drive from their home or office.

It's incredibly convenient . . . so why not?

You can hurt yourself financially if you value convenience and expediency over cash reserve yields.

A lot of consumers don't understand that the difference in rates among banks can be significant—and the banking giants are typically the stingiest. Because the large banks enjoy dominant market share, they don't feel compelled to offer high interest rates on deposits: They can still attract and retain plenty of customers without waving that carrot. (The nation's top ten banks today control about half of the market share.)

According to FDIC numbers, smaller banks pay higher interest on savings accounts and other bank deposits. During one recent year, the ten largest banks paid 1.87 percent in interest for savings accounts, whereas the littlest institutions offered 4.37 percent.

Small banks, including those in rural areas, are more motivated to set higher rates for certificates of deposits and checking and savings accounts: They don't have the huge network of branches, the brand name, or the same respect the big boys command. They need to work harder by offering more attractive rates to attract customers.

Online banks can also offer fatter yields. They don't have a lot of overhead (no bank lobbies to clean), so Internet bankers can pass along higher rates.

Of course, you'll want to make sure that any bank, online or not, is covered by FDIC insurance. To check, call the FDIC's Division of Compliance and Consumer Affairs (877-275-3342) or use the FDIC's Bank Find feature at www.fdic.gov.

To compare rates among banks, check www.bankrate.com. Reserve -bank.com also provides links to banks across the United States, and Yahoo! maintains web links to each state's banks (type "Yahoo! directory banks" into the Yahoo! search engine).

What's the Point?

Don't limit your search to the biggest banks when scouting
for higher yields on your cash deposits.

CHAPTER 15

Money Market Funds
Make Money

Many investors pay little or no attention to how they invest their
cash, thinking they will park the money while they wait for the
next opportunity and not worrying about the payout on that cash.
Over time, however, that money tends to get sticky, and stay
where it has been left, without much regard to the payout.
—Chuck Jaffe, *MarketWatch* columnist

I f you want a safe harbor for your cash that's more flexible than a CD
and pays greater yields than bank accounts, consider a money market fund.

What every money market fund promises its customers is that the
value of each fund share will remain at $1. How much profit you make
depends on the yield, which vacillates.

The $1 value of each share has been sacrosanct in the industry. The
fear is that if a money market stumbles and drops in value below that
$1 mark, investors will lose confidence in money markets and run into
the waiting arms of banks offering FDIC-insured deposits. On the
extremely rare occasion when a money market has appeared on the
verge of "breaking the buck," in industry jargon, its financial institution has propped it up.

The FDIC doesn't insure money market funds, but there's little need for concern. They've been extremely safe.

The recent experience of the Reserve fund—the nation's oldest money market fund—was an anomaly.

In the fall of 2008, the Reserve fund became collateral damage for the subprime mortgage fiasco. The money market held debt from Lehman Brothers, which became worthless when it declared bankruptcy.

Investors stampeded to pull their money out of the Reserve fund, which announced it would be forced to break the buck. The fund froze accounts; the inevitable lawsuits were filed. The Reserve fund's collapse was so unnerving that the Treasury Department aggressively stepped in to restore confidence by announcing a temporary program to insure money market funds.

Only *one* other time in the history of money markets has a fund broken the buck. In 1994, the Community Bankers U.S. Government Money Fund liquidated its shares at ninety-six cents a pop. (No retail customers were hurt.)

Money markets remain a sound repository for cash. They're heavily regulated by the U.S. Securities and Exchange Commission (SEC). Money markets invest in very short-term debt, such as U.S. Treasury bills, CDs (usually traded in $1 million units), and other highly liquid fixed-income securities.

Why should you care about money markets? In a word: *yield*.

Money market funds almost always offer a higher return than bank savings accounts, and they often also produce greater yields than six- and twelve-month certificates of deposit.

They also routinely beat the yields of bank money market accounts, which are known as MMAs. The MMA is a bank savings account and shouldn't be confused with money market funds, which are actually mutual funds. Money market funds are routinely offered at brokerage firms and mutual fund companies, like Vanguard Group, Fidelity Investments, and Charles Schwab.

When short-term rates are rising, money market fund investors can benefit because fund managers continually add new debt to their portfolios, which carries higher yields. If you are invested in a CD, you'll have to wait for it to mature before you can move money to something paying a higher yield (although some "step-up" CDs will permit you to make additional deposits and take advantage of higher yields).

Money markets are also attractive because of their liquidity, which makes them an ideal place to park cash. Invest in one and you can write checks off the account. Some money markets impose a minimum amount for checks, such as $500; others don't. Money market funds also typically allow customers to redeem shares by phone.

As with other funds, to get the highest yields, look for money market funds that charge rock-bottom expenses.

You can find a fund's fees by looking at its prospectus. A good place to check for low-cost funds is the large fund families: Vanguard, Fidelity, and Charles Schwab.

Don't be snookered by "teaser" yields. To attract customers, some money market sponsors waive or reduce fees for a short period of time and hope that when they raise them, investors won't notice. This information is buried in the prospectus, which few investors read.

If you're keen on money market funds, there are different types from which to choose.

Taxable Money Markets

These provide the highest yields, but the returns are subject to federal and state taxes. They are the most popular type of money markets.

Tax-Free Money Markets

As the name suggests, you can skip paying federal taxes and—in some cases—state taxes too, but the yield is skimpier. The lineup in this category includes national tax-free funds and those designed for specific states. The state-specific funds allow an investor to sidestep state taxes. State-specific funds are more attractive in states with high income tax rates, like California, Massachusetts, and New York. A tax-free fund is going to make sense only if you're in one of the higher tax brackets.

What's the Point?

When shopping for money market funds, look for low-cost funds from highly respected fund companies.

PART FIVE

Annuities Made Simple

Most annuities are created to be sold and not bought. In this part, I tell you which ones to avoid and identify the one type of annuity you should consider.

CHAPTER 16

Immediately Consider Immediate Annuities

People spend a lot of time configuring retirement portfolios
to hedge market risk, when they should be more concerned
about maintaining their income levels for life.
—John Ameriks, former senior research fellow, TIAA-CREF

Annuities are the least understood investment option. This is not surprising because there are so many variations of them, and the insurance industry has a vested interest in making them as complex as possible.

In the next few chapters we'll separate the good annuities from the bad ones so that you can make an intelligent investment decision.

If someone gave you a pallet of oil colors, could you paint a masterpiece? Well, maybe but probably not.

But when Americans hit retirement age, they're expected to become financial experts. They must gather up the money they've spent a lifetime saving and expertly turn it into a highly efficient cash machine that will spit out income for the rest of their lives.

This task would be daunting during any economic climate. In a bear market, it's especially difficult.

What can retirees do? Many of them should seriously consider an overlooked and unappreciated tool that can help them survive the market's buffeting for the rest of their lives.

It's an insurance product called an immediate annuity.

An immediate annuity can reduce anxiety for retirees who fear that they might live long enough to celebrate their ninetieth or one hundredth birthday without enough money in their checking account to pay for the cake.

With an immediate annuity, you give the insurer a lump sum; in return you'll receive payments for the rest of your life. You may take this in monthly, quarterly, or yearly checks.

They're called "immediate" because payments start shortly after the contract is signed. They are vastly different from deferred annuities, which are often shamefully peddled to older Americans. (Deferred variable annuities aren't appropriate for most retirees. I discuss these annuities in Chapter 18.)

Many studies have shown that buying an immediate annuity can significantly shrink the odds of dying destitute.

TIAA-CREF, a large and well-respected fund and annuity manager, conducted a study that found the odds of outliving your portfolio will drop—in some cases, quite significantly—with a fixed immediate annuity. The researchers concluded that conservative investors would benefit the most.

The study reported that a conservative portfolio (20 percent stocks, 30 percent cash, and 50 percent bonds) faced a 67 percent chance of being depleted within a thirty-year period using a 4.5 percent withdrawal rate. But if half of the portfolio was annuitized, the risk shrunk to less than 19 percent.

How much money should be devoted to an immediate annuity?

Alicia Munnell, the director of Boston College's Center for Retirement Research, believes that retirees should use a combination of Social Security and an immediate annuity to meet their essential needs, such as housing, utilities, and food. So if Social Security will cover only half of your monthly expenditures, you could buy an immediate annuity to take care of the rest.

These annuities can be especially helpful for those who retire without a pension and will have only Social Security checks for dependable income.

If immediate annuities can be financial lifesavers, why are they largely ignored? A big reason is the fear of dying early. Investors worry that after handing an insurer a wad of money, they could die—leaving the insurer pocketing the cash.

You can avoid such a calamity. You can buy an immediate annuity to cover the life of both husband and wife. You can also purchase an immediate annuity that will continue for a certain length of time, be it five, ten, or fifteen years, even if the owner(s) have died.

The monthly check amount depends on such factors as a person's age, gender, and the amount invested. The older the customer, the more generous the check.

Immediate annuities are easy to shop for because insurers will provide you with quotes for monthly payments with the fees already deducted.

The most popular immediate annuities are the fixed variety. With a fixed immediate annuity, you're guaranteed a set rate of return for your investment. The check amount doesn't change, which can be unnerving if inflation kicks in: Imagine how much your monthly annuity check would buy if a box of Cheerios cost $15?

An inflation-indexed (or "real immediate") annuity addresses this concern. The initial payout of an inflation-indexed annuity could be 30 percent lower than that of the fixed one. Munnell suggests an annuity with inflation protection because the payments will grow during inflationary times.

Other experts disagree. They crunched the numbers and found that the lower payments generated by the inflation-indexed annuity were no greater than the regular annuity payments received during the expected lifetime of the purchaser.

It's harder to find annuities with inflation protection, but Vanguard offers them.

If you're interested in a fixed immediate annuity, you may not want to bet the farm on just one. A wiser move would be to spread your cash across multiple annuities from different insurers over a period of time. Remember, the older you are when you purchase an immediate annuity, the higher your monthly benefits will be.

The industry leaders in low-cost immediate annuities are Vanguard and TIAA-CREF.

What's the Point?

An immediate annuity can help reduce the risks of outliving your money.

CHAPTER 17

The Annuity That Keeps on Giving

Most people dream about doing something great and making
a difference in the world. Here is a way to accomplish
this and be good to yourself at the same time.
—Executive from the Audubon Society

C harity is usually a one-way street. You give; the charity receives.
If you'd like to help a charity and receive something in return,
donate through a charitable gift annuity.

When you sink money into one of these annuities, the charity
rewards you with a stream of income for the rest of your life. You
receive regular fixed payments (usually quarterly).

If you're thinking these gift annuities sound remarkably like the
immediate annuities you read about in the last chapter, you're right.

There are some slight differences. With a gift annuity, you receive
a tax deduction—more on that later—and the rates you pocket won't
be quite as good as you'd enjoy with a commercial immediate annuity.
Charities don't want to compete with the private insurers.

Charitable gift annuities can look especially attractive to older
Americans who want to help out a favorite cause while earning more
income than what they can wring out of a certificate of deposit.

These annuities can also be a wonderful alternative for retirees who own appreciated stock that isn't kicking off income. The stockholder might want to sell the shares and steer the proceeds into an income-producing investment, but he or she doesn't want to trigger capital gains tax. With a charitable gift annuity, the donor gives the stock to the charity and receives regular payments in return. Part of the payments will be taxed as ordinary income, part as capital gain, and part may be tax free. Consult with the charity to determine the tax consequences of your gift.

Most nonprofits use the annual annuity rates that the American Council on Gift Annuities sets each year (available at www.acga-web .org). By using identical rates, charities hope that potential donors will focus on which nonprofits to help rather than on capturing the best deal.

If you've got a favorite cause, chances are it offers charitable annuities. Thousands of nonprofits promote them, including universities and colleges, environmental groups, cultural and religious organizations, and social service agencies—such as the Salvation Army, the American Cancer Society, the Humane Society of the United States, the American Lung Association, and the Nature Conservancy.

Gift annuities tend to be more popular when CD rates are puny. The annuities enjoy an advantage because they're age sensitive. A bank issuing a CD doesn't care how old its customers are, but charities do. The older you are, the greater the monthly annuity payments. For example, the annuity rate for a seventy-year-old was recently 6.1 percent, but it was 7.6 percent for an eighty-year-old.

Annuity rates improve as you age because you'll have less time to enjoy the cash flow. The American Council on Gift Annuities establishes the annual rates with the aim of allowing the charity to eventually recoup at least 50 percent of the original donation.

Before you get too excited about gift annuity rates, a monumental difference exists between a CD and a gift annuity. When a CD matures, you get your money back, while the cash (or other assets) you hand over for a charitable annuity is an irrevocable gift.

Many charities require that a donor be at least sixty. If a donor lives past one hundred, it's likely the charity will receive nothing. The entry age can drop to fifty if the individual wants to defer the payments. One of these deferred annuities can be an ideal way to capture an up-front tax write-off for a charitably inclined person in a high tax bracket who would love steady income in future years.

There is no limit to how many annuities you can accumulate if you can meet a charity's minimum donation, which is usually $5,000 to $10,000. Staggering your money at different charities could be wise because of the age sensitivity of the rates.

If you purchase a charitable gift annuity, you'll receive a tax deduction, though it won't be as large as an outright gift. The deduction is equal to the amount of the contribution, less the present value of the payments that will be made to the donor (and/or the beneficiary) during his or her life.

The annuity checks are taxed in the same way as a regular immediate annuity. A portion of each check is taxed as ordinary income, while another part (which declines over time) is treated as a tax-free return of the donor's principal. The charity issues a Form 1099-R to the donor, which sets forth the tax treatment of the payments.

You can run your own numbers at PhilanthroCalc's online calculator at http://pcalc.ptec.com.

What's the Point?

A charitable gift annuity can be good for your bank account and your heart.

CHAPTER 18

Just Say No to Variable Annuities

An annuity that pays a fixed immediate income
offers seniors a lot of security, but a deferred annuity
is almost always a bad idea for a retiree.
—Jean Setzfand, director of financial security, AARP

In the last two chapters you learned how immediate and charitable gift annuities can help you stretch your nest egg throughout your retirement.

Few people know about these lifesavers because stock brokers and insurance agents would rather sell deferred variable annuities and equity-indexed annuities. Both are terrible choices for almost every investor.

Variable annuities generate fat commissions. Immediate and charitable gift annuities do not.

If you have no interest in purchasing one of these expensive annuities, you can skip over the next two chapters.

If you need to be convinced, I'm giving my scared-straight presentation on variable annuities in this chapter; I'll tackle equity-indexed annuities (which are even worse investments) in the next.

When listening to a salesperson gush about the virtues of a variable annuity, prospects often bite after hearing about the "death benefit." The death benefit promises that the owner's loved ones will—at the very least—pocket the total of the variable annuity's contributions, minus any withdrawals.

If someone invests $100,000 and the account is worth only $80,000 when she dies, the heirs would still get the $100,000.

This promise is going to look mighty attractive when the market is in a tailspin. But what Wall Street is doing next month, next year, or five years from now shouldn't play into your decision.

You can't buy a variable annuity today and a year later pull out your money and recoup any losses you suffered during the past twelve months. The only ones who benefit from the investment protection are your heirs.

Variable annuities are long-term investments. An insurer will penalize you for pulling money out before a preset number of years. So when a variable annuity is left alone for ten or fifteen years, as it is designed to be, it's extremely unlikely that when the owner dies the account will be underwater.

What do you get for buying an investment that makes a largely hollow promise to your loved ones? A big bill.

Annuities are insurance products—and that layer of insurance is going to cost you. The average variable annuity will charge over 2 percent a year.

This cost probably won't mean much, unless you can see how such a fat fee can crush your portfolio's momentum. Suppose you invested $100,000 in an annuity that generates a yearly 8 percent return before expenses of 2 percent are deducted. At the end of fifteen years, your annuity would have grown to $239,656.

Guess what would've happened if you'd put that money into tax-efficient index funds, charging a minuscule 0.2 percent in yearly expenses? The cheap investment would have grown to $308,519. That's a difference of $68,863!

Salesmen aren't going to talk about an annuity's expenses, but they do love to fawn over the variable annuity's vaunted tax protection. Agents eagerly tell prospects that they won't have to pay any tax on the money inside the annuity until it's pulled out.

Here's the part they leave out: When you withdraw money from a variable annuity, you'll owe ordinary income taxes on the gains in the annuity. So if you're in the 25 percent tax bracket, one out of every four dollars of profits would vanish. Also you will be subject to a 10 percent IRS penalty if you withdraw your money before age fifty-nine and a half.

If you had stuffed your excess retirement cash in a taxable account instead, the profits would have been taxed at the long-term capital gains rate, which currently tops out at 15 percent. This example assumes your stocks did not pay dividends and you held them for more than a year and a day to qualify for the long-term capital gains rate.

This tax disadvantage will haunt your heirs. That's because your beneficiaries will be stuck paying taxes on any profit your annuity generated. If the annuity started out at $50,000 and ended with a $75,000 balance, your heirs would owe ordinary income taxes on $25,000.

If you'd invested in taxable mutual funds, your loved ones wouldn't owe *any* taxes on the $75,000.

You'd probably need a crowbar to pry this kind of information out of an insurance agent.

What if you already own an expensive variable annuity? Look for a potential escape hatch. You can transfer your money to a cheaper annuity—like those offered by Vanguard, Charles Schwab, Fidelity, T. Rowe Price, and TIAA-CREF—without generating taxes through a 1035 exchange. You may, however, have to pay surrender charges. (If your annuity is inside a qualified retirement account, you don't need a 1035 exchange to make a move.)

Beware of brokers and insurance agents eager to escort your cash to another annuity. Investors get switched from one mediocre annuity to another all the time because brokers receive healthy commissions every time they convince someone to jump.

What's the Point?

Variable annuities are unsuitable for most retirees.

CHAPTER 19

The Inequitable Annuity

Equity-indexed annuities are complex contracts that pay
investors part of the capital appreciation in a stock index
and provide illusory but superficially appealing benefits.
—Craig J. McCann, PhD, Securities Litigation
& Consulting Group

Older, conservative investors are gobbling up equity-indexed
annuities.

Why?

Because the annuity appears to deliver on the quixotic promise of having your cake and eating it too . . . while not gaining any
weight.

Salesmen promise that if you buy an equity-indexed annuity,
you'll enjoy tremendous stock growth when Wall Street is booming.
But when the markets are convulsing, you can yawn at the mayhem
because an equity-indexed annuity protects you from any losses.

If only it were that simple. The equity-indexed annuity story line
is a very tall tale—much taller than the story I recounted about Dr.
Jenner in the introduction to this book.

Equity-indexed annuities are actually insurance contracts that are
so complicated they mask their true returns and costs. Thanks to inten-
tional obfuscation, investors can't compare equity-indexed annuities

with stocks, bonds, or other investments. Consequently, they believe the hype.

Here's what insurance agents are telling customers: During good times, the equity-indexed annuity provides an investor with a portion of the market's return. Depending on the contract, you could get 80, 90, or even 100 percent of the return of Standard & Poor's 500 Index or some other benchmark. During bad times, the equity-indexed annuity will protect you by providing a guaranteed return, such as 3 percent.

The contracts are studded with language that will whittle what looks like a sure thing into a rate that can be less than a U.S. Treasury bill. The Securities and Exchange Commission sets forth the complex machinations of these agreements at www.sec.gov/investor/pubs/equityidxannuity.htm.

Most investors are not capable of understanding the way the insurance provider can legally lower your returns. If they did, very few of these products would be sold.

It's hard to ditch one of these annuities, due to surrender periods that typically last anywhere from ten to seventeen years. Bail early and you could forfeit 10 to 12 percent of your money or more.

What's truly disturbing is that an insurer can change the provisions of an equity-indexed annuity contract after you sign up. You can't be sure the deal you signed is the deal you'll really get.

What motivates the big sales push for these products is the prospect of capturing outsize commissions. It's like setting raw meat before a wild dog.

The salespeople aren't constrained by the federal securities regulations investment advisors must obey. Equity-indexed annuities are considered insurance products, so federal securities law doesn't apply. This means the annuity customers don't enjoy the same rights as someone who buys one hundred shares of McDonald's. The SEC is expected to eliminate this omission soon. In the meantime, there are many lawsuits over these activities.

I could elaborate on the dangers of equity-indexed annuities. All you really need to know is this: Avoid them.

What's the Point?

Equity-indexed annuities are unsuitable investments.

PART SIX

Mining Your Money

We all fear outliving our money. In this part, I will provide guidelines so that you can be sure this will not happen to you.

CHAPTER 20

Undermining Your Money

If we take a late retirement and an early death, we'll just squeak by.
—Cartoon caption in the *New Yorker*

Most retirees have an abiding fear of outliving their money. Much of the information peddled by the securities industry exacerbates this problem and sets the stage for a self-fulfilling prophecy.

In this section, I am going to discuss some guidelines for computing how much money you can safely withdraw from your nest egg and still sleep well at night.

Of course, just because you can withdraw a certain amount of money doesn't mean you must do so. You will want to first add up your monthly expenses and deduct your monthly income (including Social Security) to determine the difference that will have to be funded from your savings. Your expenses will increase over time due to inflation, so you should engage in this exercise at least once a year.

How much you can withdraw from savings without fear of running out of money may appear extremely complex—that's because, for the most part, it is. I will try to break it down by giving you some basic rules to guide you in making this determination.

Remember when Peter Lynch, the former manager of Fidelity Magellan Fund, was regarded as nothing short of a deity?

While managing what became the nation's largest mutual fund, the most famous portfolio manager in the country veered off from his stock-picking duties to lecture Americans on how to safely withdraw money from a retirement portfolio without obliterating it.

Lynch believed that retirees wouldn't jeopardize their portfolios if they skimmed slightly less than what their portfolios had historically generated. Using this strategy, a retiree with a portfolio of 60 percent stocks and 40 percent bonds—an allocation that's generated close to 9 percent in returns since the 1920s—might conclude that it would be safe to withdraw 7 or even 8 percent annually.

There's a problem with this simple withdrawal method. It's extremely risky. Many studies have shredded the technique. Retirees who rely on averages—especially those who retire into a bear market—run a high risk of wiping out their nest egg.

A few years ago, T. Rowe Price, the mutual fund company, starkly illustrated the hazards of embracing the Lynch approach. T. Rowe Price researchers examined what would have happened to a $250,000 portfolio containing a mix of stocks (60 percent), bonds (30 percent), and cash (10 percent) in different market environments if the owner had withdrawn 8.5 percent of the nest egg each year. They used a thirty-year time period (1968 to 1998) that produced a very healthy annualized return of 11.7 percent.

The results were startling: Under this scenario, the portfolio would've vanished in less than thirteen years.

So what happened?

For retirees, long-term averages aren't relevant. What's crucial instead is the pattern of yearly performance figures, especially in the beginning of retirement.

If the stock market collapses in the early years of retirement, the nest egg is drained too soon. If the market flourishes in those initial retirement years, a retirement account could just as easily become fat and happy.

T. Rowe Price illustrated this phenomenon quite nicely. During the thirty-year period it studied, the brutal bear market of the 1970s came at the beginning of the retirement. The plummeting market and the 8.5 percent withdrawals delivered a double whammy. The only way the retiree could have prevented the portfolio's premature death would have been to significantly ratchet down the withdrawals.

What happens if retirees start draining their accounts when the bulls are charging? The results are spectacularly different. When the researchers flipped the time periods—the bear market struck at the back end of retirement and the frenetic bull market of the 1990s appeared first—the portfolio would have observed the thirty-year mark with $1.2 million in the bank.

No one can predict the behavior of the market in any given year, much less a string of years.

In the next few chapters you'll learn how to siphon your retirement accounts safely, no matter what the market conditions. It's not as hard as you might think.

What's the Point?

Don't use investment averages to determine how much money you can prudently withdraw from your retirement accounts.

CHAPTER 21

The 4 Percent Rule

Two percent is bulletproof, 3 percent is probably safe, 4 percent is pushing it, and, at 5 percent, you're eating Alpo in your old age. If you take out 5 percent and you live into your nineties, there's a 50 percent chance you will run out of money.

—William Bernstein, author of *The Four Pillars of Investing*

In the last chapter, you learned how easy it can be to obliterate a retirement nest egg in just a few years.

While many people still rely on investment averages to determine their withdrawal strategy—a perilous practice—the financial industry has long since moved on and adopted what could be called the 4 percent solution.

If you consult a brokerage firm, mutual fund company, or financial planner, there's a good chance they'll advocate a withdrawal rate of around 4 percent. They will probably leave out the range of acceptable withdrawals: 2 to 4 percent.

If you're looking for a very simple formula that has a high likelihood of protecting your retirement money, the 2 to 4 percent range will do just fine.

I'll discuss refinements to this formula in the next three chapters.

If you're satisfied using the 2 to 4 percent range, you can skip those chapters.

What's the Point?

To keep from depleting your retirement savings, limit your withdrawals to 2 to 4 percent a year.

CHAPTER 22

Squeezing Your Nest Egg Hard

The issue of withdrawal rates is a critical one that's still evolving.
—Jonathan Guyton, financial planner

M any retirees just can't live on 4 percent of their retirement nest egg. If you are one of them, here's an option that may permit you to squeeze your savings a little more.

Don't withdraw more than 4.15 percent of your net worth during the first year of retirement. If you have a $1 million portfolio, you can siphon off $41,500.

For subsequent retirement years, you can discard the 4.15 percent figure.

Instead, each year you can take the amount of the previous year's withdrawal and increase it by the inflation rate. So if the inflation rate for the year was 3 percent, the retiree with the initial withdrawal of $41,500 could bump the next year's withdrawal by another $1,245.

It's not a huge increase, but remember: This figure is intended to provide a retiree with near certainty that her portfolio will last at least thirty years. This safe withdrawal rate is based on the market's historic performance since the mid-1920s. For those comfortable with less certainty, the rate can be adjusted upward.

This option does not work for conservative investors.

The 4.15 percent figure is going to work only for retirees who invest 50 to 75 percent of their assets in stocks. Many experts recommend a stock allocation of 60 to 65 percent.

The withdrawal rates I've discussed so far all assume you're preparing for a thirty-year retirement. Retirees with a shorter time horizon can withdraw a greater percentage of their net worth without imperiling their nest egg. (A widower in his seventies with congenital heart disease probably won't need his money for three more decades.) Someone with a ten-year time period, for instance, could bump up the withdrawal rate to 8.9 percent.

In Chapter 59 I've included a chart of recommended withdrawals for retirees with different time horizons and different allocations of stocks in their portfolios.

What's the Point?

You can squeeze a little more from your nest egg by modifying the 4 percent rule to consider inflation.

CHAPTER 23

Squeezing Your Nest Egg Harder

Not surprisingly, determining the maximum initial withdrawal rate
has become something of a Holy Grail in retirement planning.
—*Journal of Financial Planning*, March 2006

The 4 percent withdrawal rule does have its flaws.

One of the pesky quirks of this approach is that it depends heavily on the mood of the stock market at a single point in time. Suppose two couples each have a $1 million retirement portfolio. One couple makes the retirement leap. The other decides to wait twelve months.

The newly retired couple, following the 4.15 percent withdrawal plan, pulls out $41,500 the first year. During that year, the stock market drops a scary 10 percent.

Wall Street's turmoil doesn't have an impact on the new retirees' withdrawal strategy. The couple adjusts their initial withdrawal by the rate of inflation (in this example, 3 percent). The husband and wife siphon off $42,745 the next year.

The second couple retires a year later than the first couple, but because of the market drop, their nest egg is now worth just $900,000.

Using the same formula, the second couple can withdraw only $37,350 the first year.

As you've seen, the money you can ultimately withdraw during your entire retirement hinges greatly on that first year's calculation. This inflexibility can be infuriating—and a growing number of experts believe it's unnecessary.

The formula's rigidity recently led highly regarded investment advisor Michael Kitces to improve the approach using the price-to-earnings ratio as a guideline.

In his research, Kitces concluded that a higher initial withdrawal rate of 5 percent per year, with inflation adjustments thereafter, would have sustained a retiree's nest egg for thirty years—except during the 1903 market crash, the Great Depression, and the 1970s bear market.

Because retirees could have safely withdrawn 5 percent throughout most of the last hundred years, Kitces wondered if an investor could be forewarned about rough market conditions.

Kitces ultimately determined that a higher withdrawal rate would be safe as long as the stock market wasn't overvalued during the first fifteen years of a person's retirement. But what crystal ball could predict that?

Kitces research found that there's a strong link to the market's behavior over such a long stretch and the ten-year average of the price-to-earnings ratio.

The price-to-earnings ratio (commonly known as the P/E ratio) is a measure used to evaluate a company's stock price. An average P/E ratio can also be used to measure the value of all stocks in the market.

The P/E ratio is the price of a share of stock compared to the earnings per share. If a company posts $1 in earnings per share (it's not the dividends the stock pays; it's the corporate earnings), and the stock is selling for $12 per share, the P/E ratio of that stock would be 12.

Knowing the ten-year average of the ratio for all stocks in the market can be tremendously valuable for people getting ready to retire.

When the average ten-year P/E ratio is high, a new retiree would want to play it safe with a more modest withdrawal rate, because it's likely that overvalued stocks will drop in the coming years—or appreciate at a rate less than the long-term average.

When average ten-year P/E ratios are low, Kitces suggests that a new retiree could safely start with a 5.5 percent withdrawal because stocks are more likely to trend upward.

The higher withdrawal rate might not seem appreciably greater, but it could yield a 10 to 20 percent increase in retirement spending each year over a multidecade retirement.

Here are Kitces's rules for withdrawal rates:

10-Year P/E Ratio	Safe Withdrawal Rate
P/E > 20	4.5%
P/E 12–20	5.0%
P/E < 12	5.5%

When you look at P/E ratios throughout history, you can see how the strategy works.

Historically, stocks were at their highest average P/E ratio ever in December 1999: an astounding 44.2. With Wall Street so overvalued, a retiree wouldn't have wanted a withdrawal rate any higher than 4.5 percent. Of course, we all know that the market experienced a tremendous meltdown a short time later, when dot-coms and large-cap stocks plummeted.

Despite the tech crash that lingered for years, it took the market nearly nine years for the P/E ratio to dip below 20. That didn't happen until the subprime mortgage and credit crisis triggered a cataclysmic market drop in the fall of 2008.

While the 2008 Wall Street disaster spooked investors, the new P/E indicators would suggest that the time might have been ripe for a new retiree to consider bumping up her withdrawal rate to 5 percent.

If you're wondering when average P/E ratios last dropped below 12, it was during the period that stretched from 1974 to 1986. You may remember that 1973 to 1974 was dominated by a brutal bear market.

To find ten-year P/E ratios, check out Yale economics professor Robert J. Shiller's website (www.econ.yale.edu/~shiller/data.htm).

I hope you now appreciate why this tweaking of the 4 percent strategy could have helped the hypothetical second couple, who retired when the market tanked.

These retirees would have left the workforce with a smaller nest egg, but they could have chosen a higher withdrawal rate because the P/E would likely be lower too. A drop in a retirement portfolio is often accompanied by a drop in the P/E market valuation; that's especially true during significant bear markets.

The idea that a retiree with a lower account balance can legitimately use a higher withdrawal rate can be a great consolation to those who retire when the markets are ailing.

What's the Point?

By taking the valuation of the stock market into consideration, you may be able to withdraw more money from your nest egg in a down market.

CHAPTER 24

Squeezing Your Nest Egg Hardest

The question isn't at what age I want to retire, it's at what income.
—George Foreman, former heavyweight boxing
champion and entrepreneur

R igid withdrawal formulas aren't as helpful as flexible ones. People behave differently depending on the state of the market.

Will a retiree feel comfortable withdrawing the same percentage of a nest egg during bull and bear markets? Not likely. It's only natural for a retiree to cut back spending during hard times and maybe splurge a little when the markets are strong.

With that in mind, William Bengen—an icon of withdrawal research—has created a different approach to calculating safe withdrawal rates.

He calls his approach a "floor-to-ceiling" strategy. His method permits the real value of withdrawals to fluctuate with the portfolio's account balance.

He considered a retirement portfolio that had 63 percent large-cap stocks and 37 percent intermediate-term bonds.

Bengen calculated the likelihood of running out of money if a retiree started with a withdrawal rate of 5 percent and agreed to a couple of rules.

In a bull market (in which the price of stocks is rising faster than the stocks' historical averages), the retiree could take up to 25 percent more than the initial year's withdrawal. So if a retiree's initial withdrawal was $50,000, he could pull out no more than an extra $12,500. That would be the ceiling. During rough markets, the retiree would have to cut back and limit withdrawals to 10 percent less than the initial withdrawal—the floor. Withdrawals would be taken at the beginning of each year.

Bengen concluded that retirees who followed this approach had a 91 percent chance of their portfolio lasting for thirty years.

The floor-to-ceiling approach allows what Bengen considers a tolerable range of withdrawals. It is a powerful alternative to retirees who want to maximize their withdrawals without depleting their nest eggs.

What's the Point?

You can safely increase the amount you can withdraw from your retirement nest egg by taking into account market conditions on the date of your withdrawals.

PART SEVEN

Simple Steps to Stretch Your Money

You can increase the amount of money you will have in retirement by knowing some basic rules. In this part, I discuss how you can maximize the money in your tax-deferred accounts and which accounts should be emptied first.

CHAPTER 25

Basic Withdrawal Strategies

When you put $100 into your 401(k) plan, you have no idea at that moment what your ultimate tax savings from that contribution is going to be. That savings depends on future tax rates. Just recognizing tax uncertainty is the beginning of wisdom.

—Stephen Utkus, principal, Vanguard Center for Retirement Research

Most retirees have their money in different "buckets." Retirement accounts such as pensions, 401(k) plans and IRAs, annuities, and taxable accounts are the most common.

In this section, I will explain the order in which the different buckets containing your retirement nest egg should be emptied—when you have a choice. Sometimes the rules for tax-deferred investment accounts force you to take money out and pay taxes. It's important to know those rules so that you don't suffer serious penalties.

The bucket from which you start taking the money you need to live on is a critical decision that can dramatically affect how long your money will last.

Imagine for a moment that two people both retire at sixty-five with $1.4 million nest eggs. The bulk of each investor's net worth—$1.1 million—is in "tax-protected" retirement accounts (accounts that defer taxes, but the appreciation is taxed at ordinary income rates when withdrawn).

One of the retirees withdraws from his tax-protected account first. He owes ordinary income taxes on his withdrawals, which forces him to pull out even more cash to pay the IRS tab. He doesn't touch his "post tax" money until last. (These accounts are funded with after-tax money, and the appreciation is taxed at the historically lower capital gains rates upon withdrawal.) His cash ultimately runs out when he is age ninety-eight.

You might be thinking that's not too shabby, but wait and see what happens to the retiree who empties her post-tax account first.

The second retiree hits age ninety-eight with $1.2 million left.

This story illustrates that the order in which you draw down your assets in retirement is critically important. Using the right strategy could breathe years of life back into a portfolio—and may even leave a healthy balance for heirs. Ultimately, it's about smart tax management.

Here's the order in which to draw down assets:

1. Post-tax accounts

2. Deferred retirement accounts, such as individual retirement accounts (IRAs), SEP-IRAs, 401(k)s, and 403(b)s

3. Roth IRAs

It is best to drain your post-tax accounts first because withdrawals from these accounts aren't taxed as brutally.

Let's say you pull money out of a stock mutual fund that's been sitting for years in your post-tax account. Regardless of how wealthy you are, your maximum tax would be a 15 percent capital gains tax on any long-term profits you realized. What's more, retirees in the 10 percent and 15 percent tax bracket would owe nothing on the profit—at least through 2010.

Now let's contrast that with the tax bill that retirees would face if they withdrew money from the same stock fund located within a tax-deferred traditional IRA or workplace retirement account.

Deferred retirement accounts are a great way to shave taxes while you're working because contributions provide tax deductions. But the IRS extracts its cut when you finally pull this cash out. Withdrawals from these retirement accounts are taxed as ordinary income.

If someone in the top federal tax rung (currently 35 percent) withdrew $10,000 from his retirement account, he'd owe $3,500 in federal taxes and, in many places, state taxes too. If he pulled the same amount from his post-tax account, he'd owe a tax no higher than 15 percent on the profit only—not the whole amount.

There's another reason why it's best to tap certain tax-deferred retirement accounts second. The longer the cash stays in a tax-protected account, the more the account is likely to increase in value because of its tax-deferred status.

Roth IRA: The Last Bucket

You should resist tapping into Roth IRAs until last because there is no tax at all when you take it out. Zero. They grow "tax free." One of the other beauties of a Roth is that the owner never has to touch the money—these accounts aren't subject to federal required minimum distributions.

Finally, Roth IRAs are the most valuable gift you can leave to your heirs. Even though individuals who inherit a Roth have to make mandatory yearly withdrawals, they can keep the cash protected inside the account for potentially decades, and they aren't taxed on their withdrawals. However, even a modest Roth can grow tremendously, thanks to the power of tax-free compounding.

Once you understand these tried-and-true rules, it's time for the exceptions. Let's look at the major ones.

Short Life Expectancy

Suppose an investor owns valuable stock that he bought decades ago. If he sold shares, he'd owe a ton in capital gains taxes. Even though the tax rate would be just 15 percent, he might want to avoid these taxes if his life expectancy isn't long.

How come? Because upon his death, his estate will sidestep capital gains taxes thanks to something called a "step-up in basis." When a person dies, the capital gains rate for the investments in his taxable portfolio is reset at zero. So if someone dies with $200,000 worth of Home Depot stock, heirs who sold the stock for that price would owe no capital gains taxes.

If the ailing owner sold $200,000 worth of shares from his taxable account before he died and his profit or cost basis was $100,000, he'd owe $15,000 in federal taxes.

Your Retirement Accounts Are Overloaded

If you've got most of your money stuffed inside tax-deferred accounts, your tax burden could get nasty shortly after reaching the magic age of seventy and a half. This is when the federal government requires mandatory withdrawals from traditional retirement accounts. How much you have to pull out each year after you reach that milestone will depend on a federal formula.

Before or after you reach seventy and a half, you might want to strategically siphon a higher percentage of the total amount you need to meet your expenses from your tax-deferred retirement accounts. Your goal would be to withdraw some cash from these accounts during years when your income is lower, like in a calendar year when you generated considerable medical or nursing home bills that would drop your taxable income or when you know that you won't be getting other outside, taxable income, as noted earlier.

Remember, pulling money from tax-deferred accounts reduces

the amount of your required minimum distributions. I discuss the required minimum distribution rules in Chapter 28.

Another approach is to withdraw just enough money from an IRA to avoid pushing yourself into a higher tax bracket. For instance, a married couple could have had income ranging from $16,050 to $65,100 in 2008 and still have been in the 15 percent ordinary income tax bracket.

What's the Point?

Intelligently tapping your retirement nest egg can add years to its life.

CHAPTER 26

Moving Your Retirement Accounts

I find the great thing in this world is not so much where we stand, as in what direction we are moving.
—Oliver Wendell Holmes Jr., U.S. Supreme Court Justice

No matter what the economic climate when you retire, you'll want to make sure that you handle your retirement accounts gingerly. Nest eggs are fragile; they're often most vulnerable in transit.

When leaving your job, deciding what to do with your workplace retirement plan can be challenging because you have so many choices.

You could leave the 401(k) with your old employer. Or you could move it into another workplace plan if you decide not to retire after all. Or you could stash your workplace plan in an individual retirement account.

Use this freedom strategically: You could be taking a step backward if you don't make the right move.

So how should you proceed? It depends on your circumstances, but I've made it easier to sort out by highlighting the main choices for a retiree: (1) establish an IRA rollover, (2) leave the 401(k) behind with your employer's plan, or (3) cash in—sort of.

Roll Over

For most people, creating an IRA rollover account is a slam dunk. Once the money from your 401(k), 403(b), or 457(b) is moved into a rollover, it's sheltered from taxes as long as it remains undisturbed. It's an excellent way to consolidate your nest egg because retirement savings can be corralled from different jobs into one place.

An IRA rollover, which you can establish at just about any financial institution, can provide a safe haven for workplace plans that are stuffed with bloated fees and ugly investment choices. An investor who rolls the cash into an IRA can assemble a low-cost retirement portfolio with the investment options in my recommended portfolios. (You can find these portfolios in Appendix B.)

When transferring money into an IRA, don't request a check from your company. While it's perfectly legal to do so, you are courting disaster. That's because you *must move the money into an IRA within sixty days of receipt* of the check. Not sixty-one days. The Internal Revenue Service is a real stickler on this.

If you miss the deadline, you blow the tax protection. Taxes will be owed on the full amount. If applicable, you'll also be hit with the 10 percent early withdrawal penalty.

The prudent course is to move the money to an IRA by way of a trustee-to-trustee transfer. This simply means that your company will send the money directly to the financial institution that you designate.

Leave the Money in Your Present 401(k)

Some people keep their 401(k) parked at their former workplace(s), but that's usually not a judicious move. A retiree's investment choices are generally superior and cheaper in an IRA rollover.

If you're going to need your 401(k) money soon, leaving it with your prior employer could be wise. Many people don't realize they can withdraw funds from an old 401(k) without getting smacked with the early withdrawal penalty as long as they've reached their fifty-fifth birthday. Once the money is rolled into an IRA, that 10 percent penalty will be lurking until they are fifty-nine and a half.

Remember, your age won't insulate you from paying federal and state income taxes on any withdrawal from a 401(k) or other workplace plan.

Take the Money and Pay the Tax

Take your money now, and taxes will obliterate your nest egg. When cashing in your workplace retirement fund, you'll owe federal and applicable state income taxes—and don't forget that early 10 percent withdrawal penalty, if applicable. Ultimately, *40 percent or more* of your hard-earned money could easily get chewed up by the IRS.

If you're still picturing that splattered nest egg, the next advice might seem odd: Sometimes it makes financial sense to avoid escorting everything in your old 401(k) into an IRA rollover. For instance, appreciated company stock presents a special case.

Here's why.

If you stash all your company stock in an IRA rollover, you'll be taxed at your ordinary income tax rate when you sell the shares and withdraw the cash during retirement. Currently, this can be as high as 35 percent.

Here's a better idea. Ask your retirement plan administrator to distribute the shares to a taxable account.

What about the 10 percent penalty? You'll have to pay it if you haven't reached that magic age of fifty-five, but it won't be as painful as you'd expect. That's because the penalty is tied to the stock's cost basis and not its current value. If the cost basis of your stock is $8,000 but it's now worth $75,000, you'd pay $800 for the early withdrawal penalty, not $7,500.

Here's the benefit of this strategy: By transferring the shares to a taxable account, you will pay only the capital gains tax on the difference between the cost basis and the current value of the stock when you sell the shares.

The tax savings could be meaningful.

Before choosing this strategy, think long and hard about holding on to your company stock.

Owning shares of individual companies can be a financial time bomb. Ask General Motors employees. During the late 1990s, GM stock was selling for $90 a share; near the end of 2008, shares were selling for as little as $3.

Holding a concentrated position in any stock is extremely risky. Most investors would be far better off if they sold their company stock, paid the taxes, and invested the proceeds in a properly allocated, broadly diversified portfolio of low-cost index funds.

What's the Point?

Most employees would be better off rolling over their old 401(k) into an IRA.

CHAPTER 27

Roth Redux

Here's the incredible thing about a Roth IRA conversion:
There is no limit, no cap, no ceiling on the amount that can
be converted—if you're willing to pay the income tax.
—Ed Slott, CPA/author, *The Retirement Savings Time Bomb*

I f you're ready to retire, you might think you don't need any more
lectures on which is the best IRA because you're mainly focused on
withdrawing the money to live on.

But you might need to be reminded of the benefits of a Roth IRA.

Wealthier Americans haven't been able to contribute to a Roth in the
past—but they'll soon have a backdoor way of establishing one. Starting a Roth, even late in life, can be an important part of your estate
planning and nest egg withdrawal strategy.

Right now an individual can only make the maximum contribution into a Roth if her adjusted gross income doesn't exceed $105,000
($166,000 for couples who file jointly). But Congress decided to aban-
don the income limitations in 2010 for anybody who wants to *convert* a
traditional IRA into a Roth.

If your income is too high, you still wouldn't be able to contribute
directly to a Roth, but you could convert your traditional IRA into a
Roth.

To convert a regular IRA into a Roth, you'll have to pay income taxes on the amount transferred. So if you want to move $50,000 into a Roth and you're in the 25 percent tax bracket, the tab would be $12,500. The move will make far more sense if you can pay for the conversion taxes with funds outside your retirement accounts.

Roth conversions are especially attractive during a bear market. That's because the shrunken value of the assets that an investor converts would result in a lower tax bill.

There are a number of reasons why a conversion will appeal to some retirees. A Roth can be a boon to anyone who doesn't want to begin raiding their IRA when required minimum distributions kick in.

With traditional IRAs—and that includes IRA rollovers from 401(k)s and other workplace plans—the IRS requires investors to begin making yearly withdrawals not long after they reach the age of seventy and a half. Roth owners never have to tap into their accounts.

The IRS isn't interested in flushing out the cash from senior citizens' Roths because withdrawals won't generate tax revenue for the federal coffers. When you withdraw money from a Roth, you won't pay any taxes. When you tap a traditional IRA, you'll owe income taxes based on your tax bracket at the time of the withdrawal.

There's a good reason why the tax consequences of Roth and traditional IRAs differ: When you contribute to a traditional tax-deferred IRA or a workplace plan, you get a tax deduction up front. When you contribute to a Roth with post-tax dollars, you don't get the immediate tax break—which is why the government "rewards" you on the back end. In other words, you don't have to pay tax on the original contribution or the earnings.

Here's another reason why some retirees might embrace a Roth: The Roth's tax-free zone continues even after the owner's obituary notice has yellowed. The money beneficiaries continue to extract from a Roth, including appreciation in the account, is tax free. This means no capital gains or other tax will be incurred.

A Roth conversion is not right for everyone. If you need to take a distribution from a Roth within five years of the conversion date, you may be subject to an income tax and a penalty.

If the conversion will put you in a higher tax bracket, you might want to defer converting until your tax bracket will be lower, which may be when you are retired.

When it comes to dealing with IRAs, it's a good idea to consult an expert. See the notes for this chapter in Chapter 59.

What's the Point?

A Roth conversion for some high-income earners can have meaningful, long-term benefits.

CHAPTER 28

The Reverse Holdup

Required Distribution Rules

Congress wants tax-favored retirement plans to be *retirement*
plans, not estate-building wealth transfer vehicles. To that
end, Congress enacted 401(a)(9), which compels certain
annual "minimum required distributions" (MRD) from plans
beginning generally at age 70½ or, if earlier, death.
—Natalie Choate, *Life and Death Planning for*
Retirement Benefits, 6th ed.

What's a "reverse holdup"? Well, instead of someone robbing you of your money, the government insists that you start *taking* distributions from your retirement accounts.

The punishment for ignoring these rules is draconian. If you or your spouse is approaching seventy years of age, you should spend time developing a game plan for tapping into your retirement accounts.

Here are some steps you should take.

1. Understand the First Deadline

If you have IRAs, including a traditional IRA; a SEP-IRA (a retirement plan designed for self-employed people and small-business owners); a SIMPLE IRA; or a workplace plan, such as a 401(k), 403(b),

457(b), or Keogh plan (a retirement plan for self-employed profession-als or owners of an unincorporated business and its employees), you'll need to make your first withdrawal not long after reaching the age of seventy and a half.

After reaching that age, the IRS expects you to withdraw what's called the minimum required distribution (MRD) each year. You can withdraw any amount over this figure at any time, but you can't pull out less.

You must start taking distributions no later than April 1 of the year following the year in which you turn seventy and a half. Don't expect the IRS to overlook it—financial institutions must notify the IRS when a client reaches seventy.

2. Understand the 401(k) Exception

You get a reprieve from draining your 401(k) if you're still working. (If you own more than 5 percent of the company, you can't take advan-tage of this loophole.)

3. Don't Double Up

The IRS gives taxpayers a few extra months to make their first required withdrawal. You'll have until April 1 to take the initial distri-bution. But after that, you must make the necessary yearly withdrawal by December 31.

Easing into this routine can cause problems if you delay your first withdrawal until the spring. If you do, you'll have to make two yearly distributions in one calendar year, which can create a bigger tax headache.

4. Calculate the MRD

Every year, you're going to have to siphon off a different amount from your retirement accounts, but it isn't as complicated as it might seem.

Your first task is to determine what your retirement account balances are worth on December 31 preceding the year of your required withdrawal. Suppose on that date, your handful of IRAs is worth a total of $250,000. (When adding up the value of your IRAs, don't include any Roths because withdrawals are not required from these accounts.)

Next you would consult the IRS Uniform Lifetime Table to see what percentage of the $250,000 must be tapped. You can find this table in IRS Publication 590 on the IRS's website (www.irs.gov).

Let's see what the calculation would be if you took your first required distribution at age seventy. According to the table, your life expectancy is 27.4 years. So you'd divide $250,000 by 27.4 to arrive at a MRD of $9,124.

The older you are, the greater the percentage of your nest egg that you'll have to tap. The life expectancy divisor of an eighty-year-old is 18.7 years; for someone who's one hundred, it's 6.3 years.

If you named your spouse as the IRA beneficiary, and he or she is at least ten years younger than you, you'll use the IRS Joint and Last Survivor Table. The purpose of this life expectancy table is to allow retirees with significantly younger spouses to drain their accounts more slowly.

5. Be Careful with Withdrawals

The IRS won't care if you add up the value of each of your IRAs and then take the entire MRD out of a single one or a combination. The same goes for multiple 403(b) plans. You do have to siphon multiple 401(k) plans differently. If you have two 401(k) plans, for instance, you must calculate the MRD separately and take the appropriate amount from each one.

6. Beg for Mercy

What if you don't drain enough cash or forget about the obligation entirely? The punishment can be brutal. The IRS may slap you with a *50 percent* penalty for the amount you failed to withdraw. If your MRD was $30,000 and you forgot to take out the cash, you'd owe a penalty of $15,000.

The good news is that the IRS can take pity on retirees and waive the penalty if it concludes that the shortfall was "due to reasonable error" and "reasonable steps are being taken to remedy the shortfall."

You'd use IRS Form 5329, attached to your income tax return, to report the problem. If you've already filed your taxes, submit an amended return for each year the MRD wasn't taken.

Be sure to stay current with pending legislation and regulations concerning MRDs. On December 11, 2008, Congress passed a waiver of some MRD requirements for 2009. The Treasury Department has indicated that it is considering similar relief for 2008.

What's the Point?

Don't convert a reverse holdup into a real one.

PART EIGHT

Social Security and Pensions

Critical Choices

Retirees have a number of critical choices that can determine much about the quality of their lives and the lives of their surviving spouses. This part examines the most important of these choices: when to start taking Social Security and how to take your pension distributions, assuming you have a pension plan.

Security will likely grab the benefits at the earliest possible day. That's a popular strategy, but it isn't always the best move—especially for many married women, as you'll learn in the next chapter.

For some Americans, discussions about delaying Social Security are pointless. If your savings are meager, you're in poor health, or you're physically unable to work any longer, there's no need to deconstruct different scenarios.

But everyone else should evaluate their options.

The size of your benefits depends on your wage history, when you were born, your spouse's benefits, and how early you request your checks.

To give you an idea of how much money is at stake, recently the average monthly Social Security check was $1,050, while the maximum monthly check amount for those under comparable circumstances but who delayed their benefits was $2,185.

The Social Security Administration gives an example of the choices confronting a hypothetical retiree born in 1942. Here's the breakdown:

Age	Monthly check
62	$758
Full retirement age (65 years 10 months)	$1,000
70	$1,312

So, do you take the lower monthly check at age sixty-two, or wait until you're sixty-five and ten months or seventy and take the higher payments?

To make this decision easier, the Social Security Administration calculates the "break-even" point. In this example, it is seventy-seven years and ten months.

What does this mean? If this hypothetical worker knew he was going to die before reaching seventy-seven years and ten months, he'd

CHAPTER 29

Winning the Social Security Lottery

Many financial planners used to recommend taking and
spending your Social Security as soon as you become eligible.
But today, with people living longer in retirement, delaying
Social Security for as long as possible may be a better strategy,
since in your later retirement years, your payments will be
larger at a time when your other assets may be declining.
—Christine Fahlund, senior financial planner, T. Rowe Price

Когда is the best time to begin claiming Social Security
payments?

It really is a lottery. Guess right, and the payoff is pretty
good. Guess wrong, and you could be out a lot of money.

You can start your benefits once you've celebrated your sixty-second
birthday—you'll start receiving them after contacting the Social Security Administration—or you can wait as long as age seventy.

The goal is to figure out the right date to maximize the total amount
of Social Security payments you'll receive before you die.

You could figure this out with mathematical certainty if you knew
your date of death.

The reality is that most of the 162 million people paying into Social

be better off taking the lower payment at age sixty-two. His aggregate payments from Social Security would be greater than if he waited.

If he knew he was going to live past that age, he'd receive more benefits if he'd waited to claim until he reached full retirement age and started taking the higher payments.

Social Security also calculated the break-even point for this retiree if he had delayed his checks until age seventy rather than starting at age sixty-two. In this case, the break-even point would be eighty years and eleven months.

Break-even points will partially depend on the date of your full retirement age and on your investment performance. In Chapter 59, I provide a helpful chart for those born from 1937 to date.

Many people assume they'll be ahead financially if they grab early benefits, but that's often wrong. The payments are actuarially set so that Americans with average life spans will pocket about the same amount regardless of when they start payments. It's when people live longer than their peers that they can benefit from delaying Social Security.

Obviously, none of us know how long we will live, but life expectancy is one of the important factors to plug into the Social Security calculations. Your family history may provide a clue to your longevity. If you want a quick outside assessment on this question, visit www.livingto100.com, which asks dozens of questions before suggesting your life expectancy.

If you're eager to start benefits at age sixty-two, make sure you're definitely out of the workforce before you call the Social Security office. If you end up getting another job before your full retirement age, your Social Security benefits will be reduced.

Here's something else to keep in mind, particularly for those working and receiving benefits: Up to 85 percent of Social Security income will be taxed for some Americans, depending on their income.

The Social Security Administration office (800-772-1213) can help you evaluate your options. You can also check out Henry Hebeler's website (www.analyzenow.com), which offers a valuable retirement software program that examines when you should begin your Social Security benefits. Or try the National Committee to Preserve Social Security and Medicare (www.ncpssm.org).

What's the Point?

If you don't need the money urgently, think carefully before taking early Social Security benefits.

CHAPTER 30

Leaving Your Spouse a Legacy of Poverty

Each month, my wife and/or I visit four elderly women who live
alone in low-cost housing and are trying to survive on Social
Security. Sometimes they get a little help from their children.
These are very nice ladies who deserve better, but their financial
condition is determined by irrevocable decisions made long ago.
—Henry Hebeler, founder of AnalyzeNow.com, a retirement website

During a marriage ceremony, the groom commits to caring for his
bride "till death us do part." Unwittingly, many men take this
vow very literally.

There are two decisions—typically made by men because women
live longer than men—that can dramatically affect whether a widow
will spend her golden years with dignity or in poverty: (1) when to
start taking Social Security benefits and (2) how to structure pension
payments, assuming they're fortunate enough to have a pension.

The possibility of living alone and impoverished is rarely considered when couples discuss when to begin Social Security payments.
In fact, these discussions often never happen at all: It's simply consid
ered a no-brainer to take the earliest Social Security benefit possible.

Even when retirees don't need Social Security early, some men stake their claim because they assume they can invest the checks and come out ahead. Investors, especially men, overestimate their investing prowess, so it's unlikely that the strategy will work for most of them. Even if it did, couples rarely think about how the decisions to capture the earliest payments may punish the lowest-wage earner—most often the woman.

There are many reasons why women are the most vulnerable financially. For starters, they rely on Social Security longer than men do. Women represent 57 percent of all Social Security retirees—and seven out of every ten beneficiaries eighty-five years and older are women. For widows and other single women retirees, Social Security makes up more than 53 percent of their income, compared with just 33 percent for retired couples. Elderly women's yearly Social Security checks are lower than men's—$10,303 versus $13,644. Despite Social Security, 20 percent of single elderly women are impoverished.

How are husbands exacerbating their wives' financial woes? They fail to understand that taking early Social Security payments may ultimately condemn their wives to struggle in poverty at the end of their lives. (This same fate can strike men if their wife is the primary breadwinner.)

Here's how it happens: When the main wage earner dies, the widow must make a decision. She can claim her benefit based on her own earnings record or she can claim 100 percent of her husband's actual benefit. For older women, the husband's benefit is typically bigger, so she claims his. According to the Social Security Administration, 62 percent of women choose their husband's benefit. However, if the husband took the early, reduced Social Security payments instead of waiting until full retirement age, the widow will have to survive on the lower payment (unless her benefit is higher).

Married women can jeopardize their financial health by making poor choices as well.

About 59 percent of women take their Social Security benefits at the earliest age possible; only 53 percent of men do.

Why? After all, women live longer; you'd think they'd be keen to wait for fatter monthly checks. Instead, they opt for early payments to increase their income right away without considering the longer term. When men or women retirees take the earliest payments, they reduce their checks anywhere from 20 to 30 percent.

The reductions can even be more than 20 to 30 percent if you go back to work. Working income reduces the size of Social Security checks received before full retirement age. (Working income levels that trigger this reduction are fairly low).

Researchers at Boston College found that during a ten-year period ending in 2002, fewer than 49 percent of single women took the earliest benefits, versus more than 67 percent of married women.

When retiring, a woman can choose her own benefit or a portion of her husband's full retirement benefit, if it's larger. (Full retirement age is between sixty-five and sixty-seven, depending on your birth year.) If the wife waits until her full retirement age to make her claim, she could pocket 50 percent of her husband's full retirement age benefit. If she starts receiving checks at age sixty-two, she'll qualify for only 37.5 percent or less of her husband's full retirement age benefit.

Before a lower-income spouse can take any benefit from a higher-income spouse's Social Security, the higher-income spouse must have either begun receiving payments or filed and then suspended payments.

With rare exceptions, the best alternative is for the lower-income spouse to start Social Security benefits at full retirement age, for example, at sixty-six, and the higher-income spouse to start Social Security benefits at full retirement age—or even better at age seventy.

After the death of the higher earner, the surviving spouse will receive 100 percent of the deceased spouse's benefits but no longer receive the portion she was previously collecting. The same rules apply even if the surviving spouse had been collecting her own benefits.

Of course, delaying Social Security benefits requires that people have enough savings or pension income for support until Social Security payments begin.

As serious as the timing of Social Security payments may be, it pales in comparison to the decisions made about how to structure pension payments. You'll learn more about this in Chapter 32.

What's the Point?

Taking Social Security benefits too early can affect the quality of life of the surviving spouse.

CHAPTER 31

Leaning on a Thin (Pension) Reed

Our employer-based savings system is a mess. Everywhere you
look, you see mismanagement, malfeasance, and meltdown. . . .
This situation didn't happen by accident. The federal government,
with its own $11 trillion unfunded Social Security liability, has
condoned the underfunding of private pensions for decades.
—Laurence J. Kotlikoff, professor of economics at Boston University

It's old news that corporations across the country are undermining
their pension plans.

Today, $500 billion out of roughly $2.3 trillion in corporate pension assets are frozen. That figure is expected to triple in the next few
years. Corporate household names such as Hewlett-Packard, IBM,
Verizon, and Alcoa have put their plans on ice.

Chief executive officers—who have little need to worry about their
own retirements—realized long ago that they could save big bucks if
they stopped dumping dollars into their pension plans.

One way corporations tried to cover up this miserly strategy was
to replace their traditional plans with a meaner, leaner pension—the
"cash balance" plan.

Traditional pension plans give retired employees a stated monthly benefit for life. Cash balance plans calculate the benefit based on the balance in the employee's account at the time of retirement.

By converting their traditional pension programs into cash balance plans, corporations are saving huge amounts of money, because the newer pensions offer older workers with more seniority fewer benefits.

Pension benefits have traditionally risen sharply in the last few years of a person's career, when salaries are typically higher. Cash balance plans abruptly stop that trajectory by making the benefits accrue more evenly.

If corporations that offered no pension benefits had started from scratch with cash balance plans, it's unlikely that anyone would have noticed. But older workers have protested, because the companies that embraced the new pensions used them as covers as they ditched their more generous pension obligations to their older workers.

Corporate executives boldly asserted that cash balance plans were infinitely better for employees than the more generous traditional ones. The doublespeak actually fooled workers and the media for a while.

The corporate stampede away from traditional pensions sped up after the dot-com debacle. The stock market losses in the early 2000s, along with historically low interest rates, slammed pension funds.

The assault on the nation's pensions shows no signs of ending.

Here's the latest travesty: Wall Street wants to get control of the assets in frozen pension plans. Banks, insurers, hedge funds, and private equity firms are lobbying Congress to allow them to buy frozen pension plans and then manage all that cash.

Why would they want to do this?

The money managers could make a killing charging high fees to invest this money. Even better, they would have a captive audience of workers who would hardly be in a position to complain about the costs.

Wall Street's avarice plays right into corporate America's eagerness to rid itself of its pension albatross.

Instead of being laughed right out of Washington's corridors of power, the financial institutions are receiving a receptive ear.

That leaves people who represent the little guys, like Karen Friedman, policy director of the nonprofit Pension Rights Center, screaming in protest. "We think this is just a terrible idea," Friedman told *Business Week*. "In the wake of the subprime crisis, it would be crazy to allow financial institutions to manage these plans."

Despite the assault on pensions, roughly forty-four million Americans are still covered by the traditional plans.

It's only natural that many future pensioners aren't confident about what their ultimate pension benefits will turn out to be.

What's the Point?

Even if you are lucky enough to have a pension, you may not be able to rely on it.

CHAPTER 32

Pension Distribution Elections Are Critical

A good politician is quite as unthinkable as an honest burglar.
—H. L. Mencken, American humorist and journalist

The U.S. Congress is one of the many guilty parties that have conspired to make it harder for millions of Americans to retire comfortably.

Congress wasn't doing future pensioners any favors when it passed ambitious legislation called the Pension Protection Act of 2006.

This monster legislation significantly helps workers in many respects, but it cripples them in others. Here's one of the law's worst flaws: Retirees cashing out their pensions will lose tens of thousands of dollars and, in some cases, much more.

Chances are most retirees won't even know what hit them—which is what corporations and Congress were counting on.

The politicians' motivation in sticking it to retirees was, of course, to please corporate lobbyists. They tweaked the formula that companies use to calculate pensions—allowing corporations to use a different interest rate when calculating a departing worker's lump-sum payment (401[k] plans are not affected).

Historically, companies have plugged the thirty-year U.S. Treasury rate into their formulas to determine lump sums. Now companies are gradually using corporate bond rates in their calculations.

Corporate bonds have traditionally had higher yields to attract investors who might otherwise invest in super-safe U.S. Treasuries.

What's the big deal? When corporations plug higher interest rates into their pension equation, it results in lower lump-sum payments for retirees. The higher the yields, the lower the lump-sum payments.

The use of the corporate bond rate is being phased in during a five-year period. By 2012, companies will be exclusively using the less-desirable corporate rate.

Retirees can't control what politicians will agree to after face time with lobbyists, so it's important to focus on what they *can* control.

One looming question is whether to take the pension as a lump sum or as a string of monthly payments that will last for the rest of their lives and, possibly, their spouses' lives.

There isn't a single correct way to proceed.

If a retiree is in poor health and single, taking a lump sum will make a lot of sense.

If a retiree is married and opts for the most cash every month, the pension will vanish upon death. Tough luck to those who are left behind.

Back in the mid-1980s, Congress was so alarmed by the practice of cutting spouses out of pension benefits that it passed a law requiring that men (or women) obtain the notarized signature of their spouse before they could choose the so-called single-life pension benefits (in which the benefits cease with the death of the employee). If the wife balked at signing, the pension would drop in value, but it would cover the lives of both spouses.

Sadly, even this federal safeguard hasn't prevented some husbands from behaving badly. One study suggested that 41 percent of pensions ended when the husband died.

The experts at the Pension Rights Center, a consumer advocacy organization, can share all sorts of scary stories about retiree high jinks. They've heard of guys who claim to be bachelors to avoid bringing their wives into the loop. Others have stooped to using "wife impersonators" who sign away the rights of the legitimate wife to pension benefits.

Not all husbands are callous or self-centered. Experts at the Pension Rights Center and elsewhere believe that both men and women are often confused by the paperwork. They sign documents without understanding what their signatures mean.

When you're on the verge of retirement, it's important to ask questions. Too many people remain silent because they're afraid of looking stupid. It's absolutely critical to explore all your options.

In a minority of cases, selecting the single-life pension could be smart. If the husband is heavily insured or the wife is wealthy or isn't expected to live long, the husband may want to cover only himself.

Couples often have many choices if they reject the single-life pension, which should be thoroughly examined. It's typical to have pensions that offer 50, 75, and 100 percent survivor benefits. The monthly checks of a pension with 50 percent survivor benefits, for instance, would be halved once the husband died.

Compared to the monthly trickle of cash, many husbands and wives prefer what certainly looks to be a financial windfall, so they elect the lump-sum option.

The problem lies in what eventually happens to these huge chunks of money. Many couples don't know how to invest this cash wisely so that it can outlast both their lives. In fact, there may be only crumbs left when the wife buries her husband. A study conducted by the Center for Retirement Research at Boston College concluded that the tendency to cash out retirement accounts is one reason why widows are more likely to die poor.

Too many couples make retirement decisions based on this assumption: They will both die on the same day. Of course, we all know that for nearly everyone that just isn't going to happen.

It's going to be hard for just about any retiree to make complicated pension decisions without seeking help. Plenty of those who seem eager to help retirees are often just salesmen and insurance agents trolling for clients with retirement windfalls to invest. They'll urge you to take the lump sum, which often means more assets for them to manage—and more fees to collect.

You'll often find these self-proclaimed retirement experts holding "educational seminars." Avoid them.

An infinitely better alternative is to consult a pension actuary or a pension attorney. You'll learn where to find them in the next chapter.

What's the Point?

For most retirees who are married, taking monthly pension payments is preferable to a lump-sum option—especially for the surviving spouse.

CHAPTER 33

Hiring a Pension Consultant Can Pay Big Dividends

**Despite the best intentions of pension-plan administrators
and the help of computers, mistakes happen.**
—Kiplinger's Retirement Report

I f you're going to retire with a pension, congratulations. But don't let your good fortune lull you into complacency. You have something valuable, and you'll want to keep every penny of it. To get the maximum benefit from your pension, you'll need to take precautions.

For starters, become a pack rat: Keep any pension documents your employer sends you, and save all your benefit statements. These provide an estimate of what your benefit will be upon the standard retirement age, as well as what your pension would be worth if you quit your job now. Many companies automatically send these statements every year. At other workplaces, you'll have to ask for them.

Get a copy of the plan's summary plan description. This document details how the pension is calculated for the company's workers.

Don't assume your company will calculate your benefits correctly. Mistakes happen. The company could inadvertently use the wrong formula or type in wrong numbers when calculating your lump sum or the amount of future pension checks. Errors can also happen when companies merge.

Before you retire, consult a pension actuary or a pension attorney to make sure the pension figures are correct. These professionals can help you determine whether to take a lump sum or regular pension checks. It can be a very complicated decision; you shouldn't wing it.

For help, contact the National Pension Lawyer Network 617-287-7303; www.pensionaction.org/npln.htm). The University of Massachusetts's Pension Action Center administers this nationwide referral service of 640 attorneys from all fifty states. They charge on a sliding scale and provide some clients with free advice.

Another good resource is the American Academy of Actuaries (202-223-8196; www.actuary.org/palprogram.asp). This professional organization sponsors the Pension Assistance List (PAL), a network of actuaries scattered around the country who can assist workers with pension calculations. They'll offer up to four hours of free help before charging you.

What's the Point?

Check and double-check your pension benefit calculations.

PART NINE

Is Sixty-Five the
New Fifty?

In the following chapters, I offer some easy-to-implement strategies that will permit you to stretch your retirement nest egg. It will require some sacrifice, but probably not as much as you think.

CHAPTER 34

Retirement Delayed Is Retirement Enhanced

With the older baby boomers hitting sixty-two this year, and more than seventy million of them likely to enter retirement over the next twenty years, the hard truth is that only a small minority are accumulating enough savings to provide for their income needs during decades in retirement.
—T. Rowe Price study, 2008

What if you're ready to retire and the numbers aren't adding up?

An impressive stack of studies suggests that your best course of action is to continue working. Remaining in the workforce can dramatically improve your chances of eventually affording a comfortable retirement.

According to Boston College's Center for Retirement Research, for every year you stay put, your Social Security payments will increase 7 to 8 percent. You can expect the same kind of bump on the money in your 401(k) plan.

Another significant advantage of delaying retirement: For the months (or years) that you continue to work, you aren't tapping into your nest egg (or aren't tapping into it as much). This allows your retirement portfolio to grow, even if you aren't contributing to it. When you do retire, you won't need to withdraw from it for as long.

The Congressional Budget Office provides a compelling example of the increased economic power that you can capture from postponing retirement.

It took a married couple in their early sixties, jointly earning $77,000 a year. After taxes, the couple takes home $58,600 per year. If they want to replace 80 percent of this after-tax income in retirement, they will need approximately $46,900 per year.

If both spouses retire at sixty-two, they will receive (collectively) $20,100 in Social Security benefits. This leaves a shortfall of $26,800 for approximately twenty years (expected life span). It will cost them $510,800 to purchase a "joint and 50 percent survivors" annuity to cover that amount.

Look what happens if they postpone retirement. Their Social Security payment increases and the cost of the annuity to cover the shortfall declines each year they wait.

If they retire at sixty-three, the same kind of annuity will cost them $465,000; at sixty-six, it will cost them $298,400; and if they wait until age seventy, the same annuity will cost only $117,700.

If you delay retirement and simultaneously contribute to a 401(k), an IRA, or another savings vehicle, your retirement prospects will be even rosier.

T. Rowe Price illustrated that phenomenon in its own study about optimizing retirement income. The firm looked at a hypothetical sixty-two-year-old who wanted more retirement purchasing power from his nest egg and Social Security.

To reach that goal, T. Rowe Price offered this option: If the man saved 25 percent of his gross salary beginning at age sixty-two and retired at age sixty-five, his retirement income would jump roughly 25 percent. (The example assumes that the worker invests 40 percent of his tax-deferred account in stocks and 60 percent in bonds.)

Saving one out of every four dollars is going to be a nonstarter for many older workers. But you don't have to be a super saver in those last working years to significantly fatten your nest egg.

What's so heartening about the T. Rowe Price study is that even if a sixty-something doesn't save another nickel for retirement, he can still dramatically boost his nest egg simply by remaining employed for three or four extra years. Without squirreling away any additional money, the hypothetical worker could retire with approximately the same 25 percent boost in income just by working until age sixty-six—only a year longer than the example's super saver.

This financial reality could be a strong motivator for many people who end up retiring early because they want to start having fun. If they keep working, they can take some of the income and use it to pay for wonderful vacations and other splurges.

You won't be alone: It's becoming more common for employees to work longer than they would have in the past.

Over the past thirty years, employment of workers ages sixty-five and up has jumped 101 percent.

What's the Point?

A few years of additional employment can have a significant impact on your retirement income.

CHAPTER 35

Retaining Your Job and Securing Your Retirement

I don't want any yes-men around me. I want everybody
to tell me the truth even if it costs them their jobs.
—Samuel Goldwyn, motion-picture icon

I have persuaded you. You want to continue working. What if your
employer no longer wants you?

Layoffs are always a possibility—especially during tough economic times. When layoff rumors are rife at your workplace, the worst
thing you can do is to keep your head in the sand.

Despite age discrimination laws, senior employees—who are more
likely to enjoy larger salaries and expensive benefits—can be a tempting target.

It's critical to keep your résumé fresh and learn how to post it
online. You should also keep a copy of your performance evaluations,
any complimentary letters or emails from bosses and customers, and
work samples on your home computer. If you're laid off, you might not
have access to your workplace computer.

Without being too overt about it, it makes sense to remind your
employer what you've contributed to the workplace.

If you're laid off or you accept an early retirement package, negotiate for as many extras as possible: lengthier medical insurance, an accelerated vesting of any stock options, and access to career counseling.

What's the Point?

If you can't avoid a layoff, turn it into an opportunity.

CHAPTER 36

Don't Count on Age Discrimination Laws to Protect Your Job

Long-standing human resources practices invest heavily
in youth and push out older workers. This must change—
and public policy too—or companies will find themselves
running off a demographic cliff as baby boomers age.
—*Harvard Business Review*, March 2004

When today's wannabe retirees were young, employers could set age limits for new employees. A U.S. Department of Labor survey from the mid-1960s found that most employers weren't hiring anyone older than forty-five or fifty-five.

The move to more equitable workplaces began in earnest when Congress passed—nearly unanimously—the Age Discrimination in Employment Act (ADEA) in 1967. The landmark legislation protected workers up to age sixty-five, but in the intervening years, the upper age limit was eliminated. On the state level, many state legislatures also prohibited employers from treating aging workers differently.

The end of blatant age discrimination has been a good thing for a growing number of American workers. It's estimated that by 2014, nearly a third of the country's workforce will be fifty years of age or older.

Yet despite all the laws, you can still face formidable challenges if you intend to stay in the labor force as long as possible.

Why? Because the protections aren't ironclad, and they keep evolving.

In the 1970s, the U.S. Supreme Court ruled that an employer could look at wages and benefits in deciding whom to fire, as long as the decisions were made on individual cases and not wholesale. More than a decade later, the court concluded that firing someone based on cost could violate the ADEA. In the 1990s, the court decided that employers could fire based on seniority but not age.

Today, a company is permitted to hire a younger worker with less experience and a lower salary history who is willing to work in a job for a smaller paycheck than someone older. However, an older employee can't be fired because his or her insurance costs are higher, or because the company will soon be faced with paying retirement benefits.

Employment law also generally prevents employers from forcing an employee into retirement, regardless of age. While interpretations of these laws will continue to change, some suggest that the very presence of discrimination laws—and the disappearance of overt ageism—could indirectly hurt older workers or retirees seeking to return to the workforce. That's because some employers will avoid hiring aging Americans rather than risk later claims of age discrimination, which can be hard to disprove.

If you think you've been a victim of discrimination, retain an employment lawyer. (The National Employment Lawyer Association at www.nela.org can help you find a lawyer near you.) If you can't afford to hire someone, contact the AARP Volunteer Legal Review Program. Mail a detailed letter to P.O. Box 50228-M03, Washington, DC 20091-0228, or send an email to litigation@aarp.org. A volunteer attorney will assess your case.

They'll likely file a charge with the EEOC—the U.S. Equal Employment Opportunity Commission (www.eeoc.gov). Don't delay; complaints must be filed within 180 days of the alleged discrimination.

What's the Point?

The age discrimination laws don't offer any guarantee that you will be able to keep your job.

CHAPTER 37

Part-Time Work Can Be Full-Time Trouble

A curious fact about retirement behavior is that many people
later reverse their retirement decision and return to work.
—Nicole Maestas, Rand working paper, April 2007

Many experts strongly suggest that postponing retirement can
significantly increase your nest egg.

Plenty of graying workers ignore that advice: They figure
they can wing it and get a part-time job later if money gets tight.

On the surface, embracing the part-time strategy looks like a fine
plan. If you've worked in a cubicle—or worse, on your feet—for forty
years or more, it's only natural to crave a break.

A Merrill Lynch survey found that Americans who juggle work *and*
leisure—retiring but keeping a part-time job—reported feeling hap-
pier than those who permanently retired. About 45 percent of retirees who are still dabbling in the work world said that retirement was
better than expected, while only 34 percent of nonworking retirees
reported feeling the same way.

A major study by the U.S. Bureau of Labor Statistics documented
that employees aged fifty-five to sixty-four would prefer to ease into
retirement by cutting back their hours.

Before you do, consider the potential drawbacks.

If you're eligible for a traditional pension, it can be perilous to cut back hours at your workplace, because your salary during the last few years of work could affect your monthly pension checks. Your pension might be calculated on that lower pay, and your benefits could permanently shrink.

Working in retirement can also erode your Social Security payments. The government penalizes you by deducting from your Social Security payments according to a formula that remains in place until the month of your birthday in the year you qualify for full benefits.

Another consideration to planning to supplement your retirement income with a part-time job: Health issues like diabetes, heart problems, and other medical challenges may prevent you from returning to work.

Finally, once people leave their profession and try to return after retirement, it's unlikely they can obtain a salary that even approaches what they used to make.

What's the Point?

Part-time employment may not be a practical alternative.

PART TEN

Financial Lifelines for Desperate Times

Sometimes, no matter how much you plan, the perfect financial storm knocks you for a loop. The housing bust, combined with the market crash and corporate layoffs, left many Americans in desperate financial shape. And that's to say nothing of victims of Bernard Madoff–type Ponzi schemes, which have affected thousands of investors at all levels.

None of the financial lifelines I discuss in the following chapters is a panacea. Some require that you swallow your pride and accept help. However, it is important that you know and understand your options.

CHAPTER 38

The Reverse Mortgage Wheel of Fortune

Every scam artist is getting into this business. Because reverse mortgages are so complicated and give you money up front, years can pass before a senior realizes they've lost everything.
—Prescott Cole, elder-care advocate

If you're a senior and you own your home outright, you might qualify for a reverse mortgage loan. That can be both good and bad news.

With a reverse mortgage loan, you'd get a lump-sum check for the equity in your home. The loan does not have to be paid back until you die, sell the home, or move out permanently.

When reverse mortgages first appeared, most of the people who signed up were in serious financial trouble: If they didn't quickly free up some assets, they faced the possibility of losing their homes.

Reverse mortgages have skyrocketed in popularity. In 2000, only 6,640 Americans owned one; by 2007, aging homeowners took out 132,000 reverse mortgages—and the numbers keep climbing. Today, many people aren't using the cash as a final resort. Instead, they're signing on for dubious reasons—to remodel a kitchen, pay down credit cards, or underwrite a week at the beach. These are the wrong reasons to go down this route.

A reverse mortgage should be considered a loan of last resort. In the next chapters, I'll explain why.

What's the Point?

Reverse mortgages can be a lifeline, but all other options should be exhausted before obtaining one.

CHAPTER 39

Reverse Mortgages

Too Good to Be True?

We hear a lot about the concept of aging in place, and with
strong consumer protections, the reverse mortgage industry
has the chance to provide seniors the opportunity to do just
that, to grow old in a comfortable, secure home environment.
—U.S. Senator Gordon H. Smith (R-OR)

How much will you get from the proceeds of a reverse mortgage?
Probably between 50 and 70 percent of your home's appraised
value. The precise amount will depend on the following:

- Your age

- Current interest rates

- The appraised value of your home

- Mortgage limits

The older you are, the more equity you can siphon out of your home.
You won't qualify for a federally insured reverse mortgage unless
you're at least sixty-two years old. (For a married couple, both spouses

need to meet the age requirement.) Some programs that aren't federally insured will allow homeowners as young as sixty to participate.

You can get a good idea of how much money you could capture with a reverse mortgage by checking out AARP's reverse mortgage calculator at www.rmaarp.com.

For example, say a couple—both sixty-five—own a house in California worth $400,000. According to the calculator, they could receive a lump sum of $225,049 or a credit line of the same amount. (They'd receive more if they were older.) Another option would be a monthly check of $1,307. They could also choose a combination of the three payment alternatives.

The Federal Housing Administration oversees the most popular reverse mortgage program, insuring roughly 90 percent of the nation's reverse mortgages through Home Equity Conversion Mortgage (HECM) loans. Mortgage ceilings vary by county.

Recently, the Department of Housing and Urban Development approved higher lending limits for reverse mortgages. Now an HECM loan can be federally insured up to a maximum of $625,500 in some parts of the country.

Most people with reverse mortgages own their homes outright. According to one study, three out of every four homeowners seventy and older don't have a mortgage.

Homeowners can still participate if they have a low mortgage balance. To qualify, they must first pay off their mortgage. Proceeds from a reverse mortgage can be used to settle this debt.

Borrowers participating in the federal program won't be getting loans from the government. Private lenders provide the loans, which are federally guaranteed. You can obtain the names of lenders in this program by calling 800-569-4287.

To learn more about reverse mortgages, read AARP's "Home Made Money: A Consumer's Guide to Reverse Mortgage," available at http://

assets.aarp.org/www.aarp.org_/articles/revmort/homeMadeMoney .pdf or by calling 800-209-8085.

You may be thinking a reverse mortgage could be your financial salvation. That's exactly what the marketers of these loans would love you to think. In fact, they can be financial dynamite.

What's the Point?

Don't let the lure of reverse mortgages blind you to the reality.

CHAPTER 40

Making Usury Look Good

The Real Costs of Reverse Mortgages

Reverse mortgages may seem like "free money,"
but in fact, they are quite expensive.
—*Investor Alert*, Financial Industry Regulatory Authority (FINRA)

Here's why a reverse mortgage is probably a bad idea: It can *cost* you between 8 and 10 percent of the value of your home. I pulled a long list of standard fees right off the website of the National Reverse Mortgage Lenders Association.

First, you've got an origination fee. This is supposed to cover the lender's operating expenses. This fee is computed on a sliding scale based on the value of the house. It was recently capped at $6,000.

Next is the mortgage insurance premium, which can be as much as 2 percent of the home's value. After the initial hit, the customer must pay 0.5 percent of the value of the loan annually for the insurance.

There's also the appraisal; expect a bill of $300 to $400.

Borrowers will also be nickel-and-dimed by these closing costs:

- Credit report fee

- Flood certification fee

- Escrow, settlement, or closing fee

- Document prep fee

- Recording fee

- Courier fee

- Pest inspection

- Property survey

If these fees weren't egregious enough, lenders can deduct a service fee, set aside from the loan proceeds, to cover the projected costs of servicing a loan. According to the National Reverse Mortgage Lenders Association, this chunk of money can generally amount to several thousand dollars.

Still want a reverse mortgage?

What's the Point?

Reverse mortgages are a bad deal unless you have no other option and desperately need the cash.

CHAPTER 41

Low-Cost Lifelines

The least expensive reverse mortgages are the ones offered
by state or local governments. But these "public sector" loans
generally can be used for only a specific purpose, like home
repairs. Many are only available to persons with low to moderate
incomes. But the low cost can make these loans very attractive.
—American Association of Retired Persons

B efore you think about a reverse mortgage, check into the less
drastic—and less costly—alternatives available through your
state or local government.

Deferred Payment Home Repair Loans

Many states lend money to seniors for home repairs through
deferred-payment loans. Typically, the money doesn't have to be repaid
until either the home is sold or the owner moves and the home is no longer used as the primary residence. Some states require no repayment if
the borrower lives in the residence for a certain number of years.

Property Tax Assistance

Some state and local governments provide property tax assistance
to the elderly through low-cost loans. These loans don't usually charge
an origination fee and have low closing costs (if any). Keeping up with

property taxes can be a challenge even when a homeowner is still working, but they're an especially cruel burden to homeowners on fixed incomes. Some counties also offer to reduce or freeze a senior's property taxes; call your county tax assessor's office for information.

You can also challenge your property tax assessment. Check out the National Taxpayers Union's pamphlet "How to Fight Property Taxes" (available at www.ntu.org).

Relief Programs

Chasing down potential relief programs can be wearisome, but your local agency on aging can help. It can also help you find assistance for energy bills, food programs, and medical care. To find the agency nearest you, call the national Elder Care Locator at 800-677-1116.

What's the Point?

Explore less costly alternatives to reverse mortgages.

CHAPTER 42

Should You Sell Your Life?

These [insurance salesmen] are the same people who are
now knocking at Grandma's door, saying that she doesn't
need insurance anymore and that she'll benefit from
selling her policy to them at a deep, deep discount.
—Frank N. Darras, attorney and expert on insurance issues

You used to be able to get rid of your life insurance policy by surrendering it for its cash value or letting it lapse. Today, firms are on the prowl to snatch up your unwanted policy.

If you're retired and have cash value insurance, you may already have heard from life settlement companies representing investors looking to buy policies on this emerging secondary market.

On the surface, this looks like a winning strategy: A policyholder could sell an old policy to a life settlement firm for a greater sum than the surrender value.

If you do that, the life settlement company may hold that policy until you die, and then the firm will collect the death benefit. Or the life settlement company will act as a middleman and resell a policy (or interests in a bundle of policies) to institutional investors.

People in the life settlement industry are anxious to portray what they do as a win–win situation for everybody. Not true. Life settlements are only appropriate for a very limited group.

Here are some examples of when you should consider them:

- You have a terminal illness and need money to pay expenses.

- You are desperate for cash and have no other options.

- You don't have the cash to maintain the policy.

- You get "a truly terrific deal" that gives you significantly more than the surrender value of the policy.

If you don't fall within these categories, don't believe the salesman's pitch.

The industry looks for wealthy policyholders who are at least sixty-five. The shorter the life of the policyholder, the better it is for them.

The life settlement industry insists that it's simply playing match-maker for policyholders eager to ditch their coverage.

Don't believe it. These brokers are motivated by very large com-missions, which can be as high as 8 percent of the value of the policy. Guess who pays the commissions? You do.

You won't like the way these commissions are calculated. Let's say someone owns a $1 million policy, and a life settlement firm is offer-ing to buy it for $280,000. The commission is 6 percent. The broker's commission isn't calculated on the offer; it's based on the *face value* of the policy. So the owner would have to surrender $60,000 of his take. (Don't expect a broker to tell you that commissions are negotiable.)

There's also a provider fee tacked on. It can range from 1 to 3 per-cent of the face value. That could be another $10,000 to $30,000 slashed off the settlement.

Here's the real kicker: The proceeds are taxable as ordinary income.

Life settlement peddlers are so eager to collect obscene commissions that they've come up with another way to mint money. Some firms are now urging wealthy seniors to essentially rent themselves out for insurance purposes.

These third parties will pay the willing senior a bonus for obtaining life insurance and will also foot the bill for the premiums. The thought of a stranger having an insurance interest in your life may make many seniors understandably uncomfortable.

Here are some alternatives: If you can afford it, hang on to the policy for your heirs. If you can't continue paying the premiums, you can reduce the death benefit and lower the premium. If you have built up sufficient cash value in the policy, the insurance company can use the cash value to cover premiums.

Many life insurance policies permit an insured to pocket a certain percentage of a death benefit if the policyholder is terminally ill. If it's a universal life policy, you may be able to reduce or stop premium payments without jeopardizing the death benefit.

These policies can be extremely complex: If you're having trouble evaluating yours, contact a fee-only insurance advisor.

What's the Point?

Life settlements make sense in only a very limited set of circumstances.

CHAPTER 43

Help When It Seems Hopeless

**I'm living so far beyond my income that we
may almost be said to be living apart.**
—E. E. Cummings

Plenty of Americans who believe they've stockpiled enough cash for retirement end up short.

A debilitating illness can handicap a retirement plan. Unexpectedly having to support an adult child or a grandchild can be a financial burden. A Wall Street train wreck can cause havoc for everyone.

Even if you never face debilitating financial troubles, a loved one, friend, or neighbor might. Here are some ways to receive help:

1. Look for help online: It'll take fifteen to twenty minutes to complete the AARP Foundation Benefits QuickLink questionnaire that will determine if you qualify for a variety of public and private benefit programs (www.aarp.org/quicklink).

2. The National Council on Aging sponsors another helpful resource: BenefitsCheckUp (www.benefitscheckup.org).

3. Seek assistance for grandchildren: If you're raising a grandchild,

you'll also want to check out AARP's Benefits QuickLink. The children may qualify for such programs as the State Children's Health Insurance Program (SCHIP), Medicaid, or Supplemental Security Income.

4. Lower your utility bills: You may qualify for the Low Income Home Energy Assistance Program (LIHEAP), which will pay some of the heating and cooling costs for eligible homeowners and renters. You can find the appropriate state office by visiting www.acf.hhs.gov/programs/ocs/liheap.

5. Shrink your phone bill: The nationwide Lifeline program allows low-income Americans to reduce their monthly local telephone bill. Link-Up (www.lifeline.gov) offers a sizable discount when starting phone service. You should apply for these programs through your local phone company.

6. Consider food stamps: I know it sounds awful, but you have to eat. According to the U.S. Department of Agriculture (USDA), only 31 percent of seniors who qualify for food stamps enroll in the program. To find out if you qualify, go to www.snap-step1 .usda.gov/fns.

6. Try food banks: You might be more comfortable accepting food from a food bank or pantry. The charities that provide this service can be friendlier and less apt to ask intrusive questions than will the government.

What's the Point?

Seniors in serious financial trouble can find help.

PART ELEVEN

Care Costs

The most vexing financial issue facing retirees is healthcare. In the following chapters, I lay out some options for retirees who have left their jobs before they are eligible for Medicare. I also give you some guidance on evaluating long-term care policies.

CHAPTER 44

Care Before Medicare

**Health coverage is an important part of retirement security.
When people think about retirement, they often focus on
income and financial planning, but it's hard to have retirement
security without good health coverage. It's particularly
important for people not yet eligible for Medicare.**
**—Tricia Neuman, director of the Kaiser Family
Foundation's Medicare Policy Project**

A re you itching to retire—but health insurance anxiety is keeping
you at your desk?

Retiree healthcare has been a stubborn deal breaker for millions of Americans who haven't reached that magic age of sixty-five, when Medicare coverage kicks in.

The early-retiree healthcare issue is critical: Because you qualify for Social Security benefits at sixty-two, many people end up retiring sooner than sixty-five.

Healthcare for many younger retirees didn't used to be such an expensive proposition because employers—at least the large ones—often provided coverage. In 1988, 66 percent of large employers offered health insurance coverage to retirees. In 2007, only 33 percent did.

Unless you have coverage from a former employer or a spouse or you retire at age sixty-five, your options will be expensive—but that's still better than retiring without *any* coverage.

There are many ways to find retiree health coverage while waiting for Medicare.

Use a Spouse's Coverage

Using your spouse's coverage is usually the best alternative, as long as your spouse has coverage. Your spouse's premium will likely increase, but the price should be far lower than an individual insurance policy.

Before retiring, make sure your spouse can add you. Find out what the window of opportunity is for including family members. Some companies limit new policyholders to their open enrollment period for benefits, which usually occurs late in the year.

Check Out COBRA

It's possible to continue participating in your former employer's group insurance plan thanks to a federal act that's simply referred to as COBRA. (The acronym stands for Consolidated Omnibus Budget Reconciliation Act.)

COBRA sounds like a godsend, but the sticker price can be shocking. Companies just aren't generous with ex-employees, so COBRA participants pay the entire cost of the premium—$1,000 or more a month.

COBRA allows you to continue your employee insurance benefits for a minimum of eighteen months regardless of any preexisting conditions you might have. If you qualify for Medicare when you retire, your spouse can enjoy health coverage through COBRA for up to three years. Your spouse is also eligible for thirty-six months of coverage if you die or divorce.

If you have COBRA coverage, check with the insurer before moving. You may lose your insurance if you leave the insurer's coverage area.

Take Advantage of HIPAA

If time runs out on your COBRA coverage, another federal program can help. The Health Insurance Portability and Accountability Act (HIPAA) allows COBRA consumers to obtain individual insurance policies despite any preexisting conditions. HIPAA doesn't regulate the prices, so these policies are likely to be quite costly.

Look for Other Group Insurance

Coverage through a group—a professional, fraternal, or social organization—can be cheaper than buying an individual policy.

Shop for Individual Health Insurance

It can be tough to find individual policies for older Americans who aren't eligible through HIPAA.

A few insurers have developed health insurance products specifically for early retirees. One motivation for these insurers is the hope that retirees will purchase their products even after they are eligible for Medicare.

Some states—like New York, New Jersey, Maine, and Vermont—require insurers to charge their residents the same premiums regardless of whether someone has cancer, congestive heart failure, or a spotless health record. These policies are expensive because people who generate lots of medical bills can't be excluded.

Use a State High-Risk Pool

If you are shut out of all of these options, your state might maintain a high-risk insurance pool as a last resort. Some states will make arrangements with insurers to finance a pool of uninsurable Americans. The cost for this coverage will be high, and in some states you may encounter waiting lists.

You can discover if your state maintains such a program by calling the appropriate department of insurance. You can find the links for insurance regulators for all fifty states by visiting the National Association of Insurance Commissioners (www.naic.org/consumer_home .htm).

Consider Supplemental Medicare Coverage

If you qualify for Medicare, remember that it doesn't cover all healthcare expenses, which is why many retirees purchase Medigap insurance, Medicare Part D (prescription drug coverage), or both.

What's the Point?

Investigate your health insurance options before deciding whether you can afford to retire.

CHAPTER 45

The Short Skinny on Long-Term Care

After more than two decades on the market, long-term care insurance remains a tough sell. Only 10 percent of people over 65 own policies, with many holdouts saying that they are intimidated by high costs and the bewildering array of benefit levels, deductible periods, and other features.
—*The New York Times*, July 24, 2005

After spending a lifetime building up a respectable nest egg, retirees are terrified that it will vanish under an avalanche of nursing home bills.

Unfortunately, that happens every day. The cost of space in often-dreary digs is frightening. The average yearly nursing home tab exceeds $67,000; spending a year in an assisted living facility can cost more than $35,000.

With the cost of visiting nursing care rising—a home health aide costs $29 an hour—staying at home with a debilitating medical condition isn't cheap, either.

These ominous figures still haven't convinced most retirees to buy a long-term care insurance policy. Almost 70 percent of Americans over age sixty-five will require some form of long-term care, but only 10 percent of those fifty-five or older own a policy.

Long-term care offers daily assistance for those who need a bit of help to stay independent; it also provides home medical care. (Be sure your policy covers home care and not just nursing home care.)

Why do so few of us buy long-term coverage? Many people mistakenly believe that Uncle Sam will pick up the nursing home tab.

Private health insurers, HMOs, and Medicare don't pay for custodial care, either at home or in a nursing facility. (Medicare will cover "medically necessary" care in those settings if you meet certain conditions.)

Long-term care policies are complicated, and they seem to have as many parts as a grandchild's Lego set. Some of the critical questions are the following:

- Do I need long-term care coverage?

- How much does it cost?

- How much coverage should I buy?

- Should I get inflation protection?

- How long should the policy last?

- What should the elimination period (deductible) be?

- Do I need non-forfeiture benefits?

In the next few chapters, we'll tackle these questions.

What's the Point?

You need to determine if long-term care insurance should be part of your financial planning.

CHAPTER 46

Who Needs Long-Term Care Insurance?

This type of insurance is truly not a one-size-fits-all type of recommendation.
—Michael Kitces, investment advisor

D o you need long-term care coverage?

Medicaid will pick up the nursing home tab for Americans without assets, while the wealthy can handle nursing home or in-home care costs themselves.

For those of you in between, here's a breakdown.

Net Worth Less Than $200,000

If your assets are below $200,000, long-term care coverage generally isn't practical. You'd be able to exempt some assets when being considered for Medicaid, which covers nursing home costs for those with low incomes.

People in this category may still want a policy because they want access to better facilities. Someone covered by Medicaid isn't going to enjoy the same array of choices as someone who has an insurer paying the bills. (Some nursing homes limit the number of beds available to Medicaid recipients.)

Net Worth Between $200,000 and $750,000

If you fit into the $200,000 to $750,000 niche, you could potentially take the greatest financial hit from institutional care. You won't qualify for Medicaid until most of your assets are depleted. Retirees in this range will benefit the most from the growing number of states offering long-term care partnership programs (see Chapter 47).

If you have assets in this range, you should seriously consider choosing a so-called short-fat policy. (This is a policy that offers coverage for a shorter period of time with richer daily benefits. We'll discuss these policies in the next chapter.)

Net Worth Between $750,000 and $2 million

If you're in the $750,000 to $2 million category, your nursing home stay probably wouldn't deplete your nest egg. Nevertheless, paying for years in a facility could hurt the living standards of your surviving spouse. You also might benefit from a short-fat policy.

Net Worth Between $2 million and $4 million

Wealthy Americans can usually cover the bills for a nursing facility or at-home care themselves. If you're in this category and still want coverage, you might want to choose one of two alternatives: a policy with an extremely long elimination period with lifetime benefit coverage or a lifetime benefit policy with a rich daily benefit that would support a higher level of care.

What's the Point?

Your net worth is a key factor in determining your need for
long-term care insurance.

CHAPTER 47

When Fat Beats Skinny

*Choosing the Right Long-Term
Care Insurance*

Do you need long-term care insurance? Do your parents need
it? To anyone who has seen, up close, how much it costs to
care for a failing relative or friend, the answer is yes.
—Jane Bryant Quinn, personal finance journalist

Here's how to find a long-term care policy that's best and most economical for you.

Choose Between "Fat" and "Thin"

Determine the amount of benefits you want and the length of the coverage. You'll choose either a short-fat or a long-thin policy.

With a short-fat policy, you buy coverage for a shorter period of time, but the daily benefits are bigger. A long-thin policy offers the opposite—the coverage period is longer, but the policy provides lower daily expenses.

A short-fat policy, for example, might pay for $200 of expenses every day for three years, while a long-thin policy could reimburse the policyholder up to $100 a day for six years.

For most retirees, the superior option will be the short-fat policy because they'll only need the benefit for two or three years. Unfortunately, they probably won't live long enough to require a policy with extended coverage. The average length of stay in nursing homes is less than three years.

A policy with greater benefits will give you a wider number of nursing home or assisted living options. With less generous coverage, you may not be able to afford quality facilities.

You can treat a shorter policy like a lengthier one—just slow down the claims. If a three-year policy covered $200 a day, but the policyholder only claimed $150 a day, the policy would extend beyond the three years. (A longer policy doesn't work that way: If a six-year policy provided for $125, you couldn't put in claims for $200 a day over a shorter period.)

Select a Daily Benefit

You'll also have to decide on daily benefit coverage. When you do, don't rely on national averages. They're not going to mean much if you're looking for nursing home care in New York City versus Vermillion, South Dakota. (The typical private room in a San Francisco nursing home costs $274 a day; in Houston, it's $155).

For average prices by state and intrastate, check out the federal National Clearinghouse for Long-Term Care Information (www.long termcare.gov).

Should You Consider Inflation?

Probably not, because of the relatively short stay of the average nursing home resident. However, if you want to cover all the contingencies, here's what you need to know about inflation-protected policies.

Long-term care shoppers can pick between two types of inflation riders—simple and compound coverage. The compound rider provides better coverage because benefits are increased by 5 percent annually.

The difference may seem insignificant, but it isn't. Let's assume that someone bought a $200-a-day benefit for three years, which amounts to a benefit pool of $219,000. Ten years later, the benefit cash pool would have reached $317,550 with the simple inflation calculation and $339,741 with the 5 percent compounded inflation rider. Of course, without inflation protection, the policy would still be worth $219,000.

Pick an Elimination Period

A policy's elimination period dictates when benefits actually begin. You can select a policy in which the waiting period is 30, 60, 90, or 180 days or even an entire year. On the other extreme, some policies will begin without any wait at all.

You'll want to look at how insurers price policies with different elimination periods before deciding which provides the best fit.

Consider a State Partnership Policy

A growing number of states have formed partnerships with private long-term care insurers that will make purchasing policies more attractive. If you purchase a policy through one of these partnerships, you'll find it easier to qualify for future Medicaid coverage of nursing home costs.

With one of these policies, Medicaid will disregard assets you own that equal the amount of benefits you received through your long-term care policy. You can learn more about these partnerships and find out which states participate at the National Clearinghouse for Long-Term Care Information (www.longtermcare.gov).

Avoid Unnecessary Taxes

When purchasing a policy, be sure that your long-term care policy is "federally qualified," so that the benefits you receive will be income tax free.

What's the Point?

A shorter long-term care policy with bigger benefits is
usually your best bet.

CHAPTER 48

Keeping Your Long-Term Care Policy in Force

In just ten years, approximately fifty million Americans will be
over the age of sixty-five. More than half of these individuals
will require at least one year of long-term care, and 20 percent
will require more than five years of care before they die.
—Fidelity Investments research, June 2008

C an you afford long-term care insurance?
　　Buying a policy will be a waste if you can't afford the premiums.

The price tag will vary dramatically, depending on all sorts of factors: your age, the desired benefits, the length of coverage, and whether you want inflation protection.

To give you a rough idea of costs, the federal National Clearinghouse for Long-Term Care Information compiles average prices. Its latest figures are for 2005 premiums; you should expect to pay more today. (One report estimated that these policies increase in price 7 percent per year.)

AVERAGE ANNUAL PREMIUMS

Ages	Premium
All	$1,973
55–64	$1,877
65–69	$2,003
70–74	$2,341
75+	$2,604

A recent Fidelity Investments survey estimates that a sixty-five-year-old couple in moderately good health would ultimately spend $85,000 to pay the yearly premiums on a joint long-term care policy over their expected lifetimes.

Premiums are supposed to remain constant as policyholders age, but an insurance company can boost premiums for everybody in an entire class—like all policyholders seventy-five and older. At least half the states, including Florida, Ohio, Pennsylvania, and Texas, have created laws to help consumers whose premiums have risen beyond a certain threshold.

The fear of dropping coverage has prompted some policyholders to buy a so-called non-forfeiture benefit. This provision allows the policyholder to receive the daily benefit for a shortened benefit period even though he or she has stopped paying the premiums. Some insurers will charge up to double the policy price for this peace of mind.

What's the Point?

Make sure you can afford the premiums when buying long-term care coverage.

CHAPTER 49

Where's the Check?

Making Claims and Getting Paid

The bottom line is that insurance companies make money when
they don't pay claims. They'll do anything to avoid paying because
if they wait long enough, they know the policyholders will die.
—Mary Beth Senkewicz, former senior executive,
National Association of Insurance Commissioners

Long-term care insurers love new clients—but as an alarming number of elderly policyholders know, while these insurers are eager
to take the premiums, they may not be so keen to pay the claims.

Recently, the *New York Times* uncovered a variety of insurer scan-
dals, concluding that policyholders confronted "unnecessary delays
and overwhelming bureaucracies."

One eighty-five-year-old dementia patient was given the wrong
paperwork by her insurer; a lawsuit claimed the woman was denied
coverage because of the improper paperwork. Another lawsuit alleged
that an insurer tried to rescind the policy of a seventy-two-year-old
man who was diagnosed with Alzheimer's disease four years *after*
purchasing the coverage.

According to the National Association of Insurance Commissioners, total complaints about long-term care policies across the country

skyrocketed 123 percent from 2004 to 2006. During the same period, complaints specifically dealing with claims jumped nearly 175 percent.

A congressional committee has launched an investigation of long-term care practices, and the federal Government Accountability Office has started its own investigation.

In the meantime, how can you make sure you're buying from a reputable company?

Contact your state insurance regulator (visit the National Association of Insurance Commissioners at www.naic.org and click on "States & Jurisdictions") and ask about the complaint ratio for each company that you're considering. This number will compare policies to customer complaints.

Ask your state insurance regulator for the track record of premium increases for individual insurers. Stick with insurers enjoying an A rating or better from the big rating services, like A. M. Best and Standard & Poor's.

What's the Point?

Do your due diligence before purchasing a long-term care policy.

PART TWELVE

The State of Your Estate

Estate planning is not technically part of retirement planning, yet the two are intertwined. Few of us live in a vacuum. We want to provide for our surviving spouse or significant other. We also want to maximize what we will leave to our children or to other heirs, some of whom might be dependent on us even after our death.

Although detailed estate planning issues are beyond the purview of this book and my personal expertise, I offer some simple guidelines for you to consider, including wills, probate, trusts, and even prenuptial agreements for late-in-life couples.

CHAPTER 50

Find the Will to
Leave a Will

Dying intestate is like taking your property and attempting to
throw it to your heirs on the other side of a deep chasm, a chasm
which is filled with hazards. These hazards (probate, creditors,
con artists, lawsuits, judgments, lawyers, and death taxes)
can damage much of the value of your estate and allow your
property to go to unintended heirs and in unintended ways.
—National Association of Financial & Estate Planning

To die without a will can waylay your best intentions and justify your worst fears. If you die without a will—called dying "intestate"—state government agencies routinely step in to determine who gets what.

Would you really want the state to decide who gets your house or your portfolio of mutual funds?

A will is essential to establish an estate plan. It's simply a document that dictates where you want your property—your house, furniture, jewelry, vehicles, savings account, and taxable investment accounts—to go after your death. (If you're raising any children under eighteen, your will would also designate who should continue to raise them.)

Through a will, you'll also select an executor—a spouse, a friend, or an attorney—to distribute your property, pay your outstanding bills, complete your final tax returns, handle the funeral costs, and transfer what's left to heirs.

A will might sound like an all-purpose document to dispose of your entire estate, but it has its limits. You can't direct who will inherit IRAs, workplace retirement accounts, pensions, or annuities. For those accounts, you designated your beneficiaries when you set them up. That's why it is so important to keep these forms current.

Remember: If you've remarried and you had named your first spouse as the beneficiary of any one of these accounts, you'll need to change the form . . . unless you *do* want your first spouse to inherit your 401(k).

What's the Point?

You need a will, but you should understand its limitations.

CHAPTER 51

Avoiding Probate Purgatory

A man's dying is more the survivors' affair than his own.
—Thomas Mann, German novelist

Most people probably couldn't tell you what goes on in a probate court, but they've heard enough to want to keep their distance. Probate court will determine whether a deceased person's will is legitimate. The process can be arduous, lengthy, and expensive, costing 5 percent or more of an estate's value. Often the big winners are the estate lawyers.

In probate court, the deceased's property is inventoried. The court also oversees paying off the deceased person's debts and distributing what's left to heirs. If a person dies without a will, the probate court selects an administrator and determines who gets the assets based on state law. (Under many state laws, probate court records are public.)

Here's how to keep your loved ones from dealing with probate court.

Create a Living Trust
A will is a document with your wishes listed; a living trust contains the assets you want to leave for your heirs. During your life, you control and administer the trust. Upon your death, your wishes will be carried out by your trustee. This kind of trust is revocable. You can

change your directions to the trustee or revoke the entire trust whenever you want. You can also add assets to the trust and take assets out of it any time you want.

By creating a living trust, you'll sidestep probate court for those assets that are in the trust. The trust owns the assets, not you. When you die, there's no need for probate.

It can be a hassle to establish a living trust. All the accounts and any property (such as the family home) placed inside must be re-titled, reflecting that a trust now owns those assets.

Married couples can establish a joint living trust. When the surviving spouse dies, the assets would sidestep probate.

For married couples, a living trust can be tailored to avoid or reduce estate taxes. When creating the trust, an estate attorney can make sure that it includes language for an "exemption equivalent" or "bypass trust."

The exemption equivalent provision ensures that each spouse will claim his or her estate tax credit. In 2009, the estate tax exempt amount is $3.5 million. So if a couple is worth $7 million, and they each claim $3.5 million through the use of an exemption equivalent trust, no estate tax will ultimately be owed.

Name a Beneficiary for Retirement Accounts

It's very easy to avoid probate court with retirement accounts: Just make sure you've named one or more beneficiaries for each one. (Your financial institution can tell you if you filled out the paperwork for this when you opened the account.) When you die, the beneficiaries will receive the accounts without any probate involvement. You could even name your living trust as the beneficiary.

Establish Payable-on-Death Accounts

It's just as simple to protect cash that you've stashed in banks, credit unions, and savings and loans from a probate court's reach: Add a payable-on-death designation to your current accounts. You'll fill out paperwork at your financial institution to name one or more beneficiaries, and you can change beneficiaries at any time. They won't be able to claim your money while you're alive.

After a death, it's easy to claim the cash. All the beneficiary has to produce is proof of his or her identity and a certified copy of the death certificate.

Create a Transfer-on-Death Registration

Set up transfer-on-death registrations for your taxable stocks, bonds, and brokerage accounts. Just contact your brokerage firm, mutual fund company, or financial advisor to get the paperwork to register your taxable accounts in what's called "beneficiary form." If you hold individual stock or bond certificates, you must request new certificates that show that you own the securities in beneficiary form.

A beneficiary has no right to the securities until the owner's death, and you're free to drop or change beneficiaries, close the account, or use the assets any way you wish. Each beneficiary will inherit an equal share of the assets unless you specify a different split. (Some institutions will only allow equal divisions.)

A transfer-on-death account differs from a joint account with "rights of survivorship." With a right of survivorship, all owners must consent to cashing out or reregistering the account. The account is also subject to claims of creditors of both owners.

With a transfer-on-death account, the beneficiary has no rights to the account, and the owner retains complete control over it.

Transferring Ownership of a Vehicle

In some states, you can name a beneficiary for your vehicle. You'll need an ownership certificate that is part of a beneficiary form. The person named as the eventual owner has no right to the vehicle as long as you are alive. It also doesn't prevent you from selling the car, donating it to charity, or giving it to someone else.

What's the Point?

You can set up your estate plan to avoid probate court.

CHAPTER 52

The Magic Power of an Inherited IRA

In many if not most cases, the biggest advantage of the Roth IRA is that the heirs receive income-tax-free distributions for their entire lives.
—James Lange, CPA, attorney, and author

What if you could leave an inheritance worth many times the value of your assets? In this chapter I will show you precisely how you can do just that, using the magic power of an inherited individual retirement account (IRA).

We all hope our children and grandchildren will remember us fondly. If you believe in the belt-and-suspenders approach, consider increasing the odds in your favor by leaving them a large inheritance.

You don't have to be wealthy to pass along a tremendously valuable gift to your loved ones.

Give them your IRA. Even a modest IRA can grow into a windfall for anyone lucky enough to inherit one.

To understand the benefits of an inherited IRA, you need to appreciate what it's capable of doing.

Let's suppose that a forty-five-year-old man inherits a $50,000 IRA from his mother. Rather than cashing in and paying income tax, he stretches his required withdrawals over the next 38.8 years (his life expectancy, according to the IRS). If the IRA grew at an average annual rate of 8 percent, he'd pull out $303,113 before the IRA was exhausted.

A large inherited IRA is an even more impressive cash machine. If the same hypothetical son inherited a $500,000 IRA, he'd siphon off an eye-popping $3,031,136 before it was finally drained. A grandchild who inherited that IRA and took withdrawals over *her* life expectancy would make that $3 million look like small change.

The longest period of time that an inherited IRA can be stretched is 82.4 years. A newborn will get this much time to empty an IRA.

The numbers are amazing because the recipients let the IRAs do what they do best—happily compound for many years.

Unfortunately, many people who inherit an IRA make a terrible decision: They cash it in, pay the taxes, and then eventually return to griping about how they wish they had more money.

If you expect to leave one or more IRAs to family, explain the benefits of keeping the account for as long as possible. Your heirs may be more likely to resist pilfering the windfall if they understand the value of an inherited IRA.

Here are other ways to increase the chances that your loved ones will squeeze the most from any retirement accounts you leave behind.

Name the Correct Beneficiaries

When you established an IRA at a financial institution, you filled out an IRA beneficiary form, which dictates who receives the cash inside this account when you die.

Failing to update the beneficiary form can be disastrous. If you never removed a former spouse from your IRA, for example, your ex will collect the money. The same thing can happen if you established an IRA before getting married. If you named your parents or siblings and never changed the designation, your wife or husband is out of luck. Your will won't save your spouse from this mistake.

To avoid irrevocable mistakes, add this to your to-do list: Contact your financial institution(s) and ask for copies of your IRA beneficiary forms (and complete new ones, if necessary). Keep the documents in your estate-planning files.

Don't Fumble an IRA Handoff

Trying to discern the logic in great swaths of the IRS code can drive you into therapy. Here's one of the code's great head-scratchers: If someone inherits your IRA, he or she must leave the original owner's name on the account. If the recipient substitutes his or her own name, the IRS can consider the IRA cashed out and taxable.

The recipient—unless it's your spouse—also can't move this money into his or her preexisting IRA.

Beneficiaries must be careful if they wish to move their parent's IRA. Their parent's financial institution may suggest cutting them a check, but if they cash the check, the IRS will conclude that the IRA has been distributed.

Roll Cash into an IRA

When leaving your job, roll your 401(k) into an IRA. If funds are in an IRA, children and grandchildren who inherit this money can stretch their withdrawals over their lifetimes. If the money remains in a 401(k), this is not the case.

The exception to this rule: A spouse can transfer inherited 401(k) money into his or her own IRA.

Convert to a Roth

If you are going to leave behind an IRA, the best parting gift is a Roth IRA. The inheritors of a Roth will have to make yearly withdrawals, but they won't pay *any* taxes on the withdrawal. This is in contrast to what happens with a traditional IRA, as discussed in the last point, in that those who inherit a traditional IRA must include the cash distribution they take as part of their gross income for that year and pay ordinary income tax on this amount.

What's the Point?

You can enhance the lives of your loved ones significantly by leaving them an IRA . . . and the knowledge of how to deal with it.

CHAPTER 53

Irrevocable Trusts Require Trust

I think we may safely trust a good deal more than we do.
—Henry David Thoreau

rrevocable trusts last forever unless the beneficiary consents to a change. Once you transfer assets to an irrevocable trust, you lose all of your rights of ownership or control.

Why do it? Primarily for estate tax reasons. Assets in an irrevocable trust are not part of a taxable estate. Income from the asset is generally immune from income tax, as long as the person who transferred the asset does not receive the benefits.

Irrevocable trusts are often used during a second marriage: A widow or widower may enjoy the income generated from a late spouse's assets, but the estate will ultimately end up with the deceased's children. These trusts are also set up for minor children, disabled adult children, or other heirs.

Irrevocable trusts are also used for asset protection. Assets in a properly drafted irrevocable trust cannot be attached by creditors of the person who transferred ownership of the assets in the trust. Many states require you to part with all ownership of the assets in the trust, including the right to income, in order for those assets to be protected from creditors. In those states, you will need to rely on the discretion of the trustee to distribute funds to you.

Consult an attorney before signing any trust documents. Remember, somebody is going to have to administer this trust. This responsibility could last for many, many years.

Trusts need trustees—often, family members or friends or corporate trustees, such as a bank, brokerage firm, or trust company. Sometimes an individual trustee is paired with a corporate one.

Trustees must oversee the dispersal of money from a trust. The trustees must also oversee how the money inside a trust is managed.

Often a relative isn't going to know how to manage a trust. It's highly unlikely that he or she is going to know what the Prudent Investor Rule is, but anybody who serves as a trustee is supposed to follow its mandate.

Here are some of its main points.

Diversify

A trust portfolio should be diversified among stocks, bonds, and cash. Before the Prudent Investor Rule came along, trustees evaluated each investment in isolation. Consequently, more volatile investments, such as small-cap stocks or foreign stocks, were often avoided because they seemed too risky.

Nobel laureates and others have convincingly shown that investing in a number of different asset classes is prudent because it can provide greater returns based on the amount of risk an investor is willing to accept. Sure, a small-cap stock by itself might be too risky, but when small-cap stocks are combined with large-cap stocks, foreign stocks, and government bonds, the risks can drop while the potential rewards increase.

Invest for Total Return

Many trustees continue to invest the old-fashioned way. They load up portfolios with investments, mostly bonds that spin off income.

The income is skimmed off and distributed to heirs. When a trust is primarily invested in bonds or cash, there is little opportunity for it to grow for the beneficiaries.

Pinch Pennies

A trustee is required to avoid any transaction costs, fees, and any other expenses that are unnecessary. An excellent way to sidestep egregious charges—and many trusts are larded with high fees—is to use index funds.

Overseeing a trust is complicated, but handing the responsibility over to a corporate trustee can be extremely expensive. The fees that some financial institutions charge for overseeing trusts can be outrageous, and banks aren't inclined to let beneficiaries move the accounts elsewhere.

Read more about trusts at Fiduciary360 (www.fiduciary360.com). The firm provides training for trustees and maintains contact information for those who have completed its programs.

Here's the bottom line: It's a lot easier to create a trust than to make sure it runs smoothly after you're gone. You should put as much effort into ensuring the future health of a trust as you do in thinking through whether you need one in the first place.

What's the Point?

Before establishing an irrevocable trust, carefully consider who will manage the assets.

CHAPTER 54

I Love You, but Let's Sign on the Dotted Line

Prenups for Seniors

There's only one way to have a happy marriage, and as soon as I learn what it is I'll get married again.
—Clint Eastwood, actor and director

If you're an older bride or groom, your children (of any age) might not be thrilled at the prospect of their parent remarrying. Because couples are often worth more when they marry late in life, you'll both want to make sure provisions have been made for your heirs.

The future bride and groom can avoid familial disharmony by signing a prenuptial agreement. It may be easier for older couples to discuss a prenup than younger couples because it fits in with the larger need for estate planning. Prenuptial agreements can make couples more comfortable about getting married and commingling their assets. They can also be used to protect one spouse when the other is strapped with such financial obligations as college tuition, child support, and caring for elderly parents.

Older couples typically rely on prenuptial agreements to ensure that both partners can take care of their own children financially when

they die. Most prenuptials limit or waive the other's right to a statu-
tory share of each estate. This can be important. Without a prenup, the
state may give your spouse certain rights in your assets at your death,
regardless of how they are titled, what your will or trust says, or how
your beneficiary designations have been completed.

If you're interested in a prenup, keep these factors in mind:

Be Honest

Long before you reach the stage of hammering out the provisions,
share your financial history with each other: bank statements, credit
reports, investment accounts, life insurance policies, loans, real estate
valuations, and credit card balances. Exchange several years' worth of
tax returns and, if there is a business involved, share corporate returns,
too. Even if you don't feel the need for a prenuptial, being honest about
finances before the wedding is important.

Don't Try This on Your Own

If you want a binding agreement, you should each hire an attorney
experienced with prenuptials. Often one lawyer will draft a prenuptial and the other attorney will review it for possible changes. You can
keep the attorneys' billable hours down if you and your partner draft
an informal agreement first. (For help, read Katherine Stoner's *Prenuptial Agreements: How to Write a Fair and Lasting Contract*.)

Don't Sign a Bad Document

It's pointless to agree on a flawed document that a judge would dis-
miss, so don't insert provisions that violate state or federal law. One attorney tells the story of a couple who wanted to include a provision that if
either the husband or the wife required long-term care, the infirm person would be responsible for his or her own medical tab. Any payments
that the healthy spouse decided to make would have been considered a
loan. It's not likely that a judge would have enforced this arrangement.

Never Forget What's in the Document

You'll sabotage your prenup if you ignore its provisions. For instance, if you want your children to inherit your estate, don't title an asset with a right of survivorship. If you do that, your surviving spouse—not your children—will receive those assets.

File the Prenup in the Right Place

Each partner should keep a signed copy of an original with his or her estate-planning documents.

What's the Point?

A prenuptial agreement can serve to resolve financial conflicts
when older couples marry.

PART THIRTEEN

Wolves in Sheep's Clothing

Losing your money in the market is bad enough. Being scammed out of it is far worse. In the following chapters, I provide rules to keep you safe from con artists, whether they graduated from an Ivy League school or from the college of hard knocks.

CHAPTER 55

Mail-Order Experts

Individuals may call themselves "senior specialists" to
create a false level of comfort among seniors by implying a
certain level of training on issues important to the elderly.
But the training they receive is often nothing more than
marketing and selling techniques targeting the elderly.
—"Senior Investor Alert," North American Securities
Administrators Association

Beware of senior "experts": people who will eagerly hand you their business cards, embossed with designations like "certified senior advisor," "certified retirement financial advisor," or "registered financial gerontologist."

These experts are trying to capitalize on the retirement boom—one American turns fifty every seven seconds—without devoting the time needed to become true professionals. You need only to write a check and perhaps complete a few days' work to "earn" one of these financial designations.

Why are they so eager to serve you? Retirees have more than $8.5 trillion in assets. That is a big pot of gold. If these advisors can convince you to turn your share over to them, it represents a lot of fees.

The North American Securities Administrators Association, which represents the investment regulators in all fifty states, issued an alert urging older investors to carefully check the credentials of anyone who claims to be a senior specialist.

Many of these specialists want to sell retirees exorbitantly priced, high-commission insurance products seniors rarely need—such as equity-indexed annuities and deferred variable annuities. The *New York Times* reported on a Massachusetts insurance agent whose business took off after he became a certified senior advisor—a designation earned after paying about $1,100 for a correspondence course. A year after he received that credential, he pocketed $720,000 worth of commissions from insurance companies through sales to retirees.

You should avoid these salespeople.

What's the Point?

Don't be impressed by salesmen touting obscure designations.

CHAPTER 56

Expensive Free Meals

**Investors should never lose sight that the goal
of the seminar is to sell them products.
—Mark Story, spokesman, U.S. Securities
and Exchange Commission**

How can you avoid dubious "senior specialists"?

You'll often find them behind microphones at radio and television stations and yakking away at financial seminars.

Let's look at some of the dangers.

Very few listeners understand that the airwaves are for sale. People assume radio stations handpick financial experts to pontificate on the air, but many local shows are essentially up for bid at radio stations throughout the country. Ambitious stockbrokers, insurance agents, and financial planners can rent regular time on radio stations to attract new clients or to sell newsletters or other financial products. In the radio industry, these are called *brokered shows*.

To play it safe, don't hand over your nest egg to anyone who buys radio airtime. It's just not worth the risk.

The same admonition goes for financial "professionals" who promote themselves through television infomercials. The products hawked on television tend to be expensive and of dubious value—like stock trading systems, real estate investing strategies, and precious metals.

Financial seminars are another breeding ground for dangerous investment advice. Chances are you've received invitations in the past from stockbrokers, insurance agents, and others trolling for new clients. (Financial firms often buy mailing lists targeted to certain demographics; that's how they got your name.) Sponsors of seminars also advertise in local newspapers, through mass emails, and on websites.

Stockbrokers, insurance agents, and planners can also talk their way into workplaces. Putting their credentials in the best light, these professionals cajole human resource departments into allowing them to make complimentary presentations. Plenty of HR managers perk up when they hear the word *free*.

Weaseling into a workplace is like striking gold; the audience is filled with potential clients. Employees are more receptive to the sales pitch because they mistakenly assume that it's endorsed by their employer.

The most vulnerable audience members are often employees preparing to retire. The seminar hosts salivate at these prospects, because these employees are often on the verge of collecting some serious cash through a 401(k), a 403(b), or some other retirement plan.

Of course, the seminar hosts would love nothing better than for their listeners to roll their retirement nest eggs into accounts at their firms.

Brokers and insurance agents also reel in victims by offering free meals at upscale restaurants, hotels, retirement communities, and country clubs. Some sponsors even entice attendees by offering door prizes.

It's not hard to find retirees who've been misled by a fast talker they met over free lasagna. In 2007, federal and state regulators examined 110 securities firms that offered complimentary financial sessions that included a free lunch. The analysts determined that most were sales presentations; some of these "seminars" included outrageous claims that they could generate eye-popping returns.

The investigators concluded that 10 percent of the presentations were actually fraudulent.

What's the Point?

If a financial professional is offering you a free meal, run.

CHAPTER 57

Whom Can You Trust?

I have been a stockbroker for five years and have made people money, but I always lose in the end. I have taken huge risks with my clients, I have lost millions, but I am tired of looking for new clients.
—Anonymous stockbroker

When you retire, you'll have to make tough decisions about all sorts of issues: Social Security, pension payouts, and your nest egg withdrawal strategy. If these decisions seem daunting, you should seriously consider finding a reputable investment advisor.

But how do you find the best qualified advisor?

Limit your search to fiduciaries. Fiduciaries are required to exhibit the highest form of trust, fidelity, and confidence. They must act in the best interest of their clients at all times. It's a very high standard, but one that's critical for the person you entrust with your life savings.

What's wrong with a broker? They're not fiduciaries. Rather than making your needs paramount, a broker is bound to do what's best for his firm first. Consequently, the potential for mischief is huge.

Here's one example of how this hidden conflict can play out: A significant number of brokers earn a living that heavily depends on the assets they accumulate. So let's suppose that a retiring worker is agonizing about whether she should stick with a pension that would generate monthly checks for the rest of her life or capture the lump sum.

For the broker, the answer is clear. If his client selects the cash option, his brokerage firm will benefit financially, because the broker will generate fees from managing the cash and the investments he recommends to the client. The retiree would likely have been better off with the monthly checks.

A simple way to determine if a financial professional is a fiduciary is to ask him to sign a document that states that he will always act as a fiduciary on your behalf. A broker or insurance agent will not be able to sign the document.

Your best bet is to stick with a registered investment advisor, who is required to act as a fiduciary.

Besides searching for fiduciaries, look for advisors who charge a fee rather than those who depend on commissions. If you use a fee-only advisor, the charges should be totally transparent and set forth in a written agreement.

Fee-only advisors will charge a percentage of your investable assets to manage your money—or they could charge a yearly retainer, a flat fee, or by the hour.

To find fee-only fiduciary advisors in your area, check out the National Association of Personal Financial Advisors (NAPFA; www .napfa.org). To qualify for NAPFA, a planner must have provided comprehensive financial advice to clients for at least three years without accepting commissions.

It's standard for advisors to offer a complimentary get-acquainted session. Take advantage of this offer. You should also attend the meeting with a set of questions, available on NAPFA's website (www.napfa .org/tips_tools/index.asp) by clicking on the "Financial Advisor Diagnostic" and the "Financial Advisor Checklist."

At the get-acquainted session, ask the advisor if his focus is on asset allocation and a globally diversified portfolio of low-cost index or passively managed funds for your portfolio. Ask if he believes he can beat the markets by picking actively managed mutual funds.

Also, check to see if he considers immediate annuities from low-cost providers (where appropriate).

Here are the right answers. If you don't get them, pass on the advisor and find someone who will give them to you.

The primary focus should be on the right asset allocation for your investment objectives and tolerance for risk.

Investment recommendations should *not* include any actively managed mutual funds, individual stocks, or individual bonds (except for very wealthy investors, where a laddered bond portfolio *might* be appropriate). Instead, advisors should recommend *only* low-cost index funds from major fund families or passively managed funds from Dimensional Fund Advisors. (Full disclosure: I recommend portfolios of funds managed by Dimensional Fund Advisors to my clients.)

The advisor *should* consider whether an immediate annuity from a provider like Vanguard or TIAA-CREF is suitable for your needs.

The horrific scandal involving Bernard Madoff raised some other red flags. Your advisor should not be the custodian of your assets. All checks should be made out to and deposited directly by you with a well-known independent custodian, like Charles Schwab, Fidelity, or TD Ameritrade. You should be able to check all aspects of your account 24/7 on the website of the custodian.

Never make a check payable to an advisor or advisory firm.

If Madoff's hapless clients had taken these basic precautions, he never could have scammed them out of their money.

Before selecting an advisor, check out his ADV form. On the form, you'll find information regarding education; professional background; any disciplinary problems, lawsuits, or arbitration proceedings; potential conflicts of interest; investment philosophy; and method of payment. You can find ADV forms for advisors on the Securities and

Exchange Commission's website (www.adviserinfo.sec.gov/iapd/content/search/iapd_orgsearch.aspx).

What's the Point?

If you need financial advice, stick with a fiduciary who makes no effort to beat the markets and who uses a well-known, independent custodian.

PART FOURTEEN

Where's the Beef?

In this part, I summarize the essence of this book into ten essential rules to follow that will keep you on the right track to a successful retirement. If you wish to delve deeper into some of the issues raised in the book, I have provided the sources for my advice, together with some additional observations you may find helpful.

CHAPTER 58

Ten Golden Rules

Practicing the Golden Rule is not a sacrifice; it is an investment.
—Author unknown

The Ten Golden Rules that I've put forth here won't work for everyone, but they should be considered by all investors, regardless of your age, whether you are currently planning for retirement or are already retired.

1. If you have an account with a brokerage firm, close it. I can't think of any reason to do business with a broker. They can't pick outperforming stocks or mutual funds. They can't time the markets. They are expensive. They are *not* fiduciaries.

2. Never buy an individual stock or an individual bond, with the exception of Treasury bills. Your expected return with individual stocks and bonds is the same as an index of comparable stocks or bonds, but your risk is vastly increased.

3. If you need help coming up with a financial plan, use a fee-only financial planner (or a certified public accountant) who charges an hourly or a flat fee and who limits advice to preparing a plan and answering your questions.

4. If you need assistance in making investment decisions, use a registered investment advisor who focuses on your asset allocation and who recommends investing *only* in a globally diversified portfolio of low-cost index, passively managed stock and bond funds, or in an immediate annuity, where appropriate. Ask the advisor to confirm in writing that she will act as a fiduciary in all her dealings with you.

5. Be sure your funds are held at an independent, well-known custodian, like Charles Schwab, Fidelity Investments, or TD Ameritrade. Make all checks payable only to the custodian and ensure that you receive account statements directly from the custodian.

6. If you are investing on your own, use a well-known fund family, such as Vanguard, Fidelity, T. Rowe Price, or Charles Schwab. Consider one of my recommended portfolios (see Appendix B).

7. Avoid alternative investments like hedge funds, limited partnerships, and private equity deals.

8. Add up your monthly expenses. Deduct the amount of your Social Security and other income you can count on. Consider purchasing an immediate annuity directly from a low-cost provider such as Vanguard or TIAA-CREF for the difference. You can now sleep well knowing that you have enough money to meet your monthly expenses.

9. Keep funds sufficient to meet two years of living expenses in an FDIC-insured savings account, a certificate of deposit, Treasury bills, or a money market fund from a major fund family.

10. Prepare a will. A will is the first important step in estate planning.

Sometimes intelligent retirement planning can seem overwhelming. However, these basic rules are really quite easy to implement.

You now have the knowledge to do it. Don't let anyone cause you to stray from the path toward a successful retirement.

CHAPTER 59

The Proof Is in the Pudding!

ROD TIDWELL: Anyone else would have left you by now,
but I'm sticking with you. And if I have to ride your ass
like Zorro, you're gonna show me the money.
—*Jerry Maguire*, a 1996 American film

I t's easy to make bold claims. Backing them up is another story.

If I called this chapter a bibliography, many of you wouldn't read it. If you found my recommendations persuasive, you may not need to read it. Nevertheless, it's important to know that there is meaningful and substantive support for my views.

If you want to delve deeper, I encourage you to read on.

Introduction: The (Tall) Tale of Dr. Ivan Jenner

I invented the story of the engineer I called Dr. Ivan Jenner, but some of the facts in this tale are historically accurate.

The surname *Jenner* was originally the name for a military engineer. The name may be derived from the German *Januarius*.

The Universität Karlsruhe is one of the oldest and most prestigious technical universities in Germany.

You can learn more about the history of Otis by visiting its website (www.otisworldwide.com).

Part One: Rethink Retirement Investing

Chapter 1: Deflating Inflation

According to the National Coalition on Health Care, in 2008, total national health expenditures were expected to rise 6.9 percent—two times the rate of inflation. See www.nchc.org/facts/cost.shtml.

For historical inflation statistics and commentary on inflation, go to www.inflationdata.com.

The landmark research mentioned in this chapter was published in *AAII Journal*'s February 1998 issue. Known informally as "the Trinity Study," the official title is "Retirement Savings: Choosing a Withdrawal Rate That Is Sustainable" by Philip L. Cooley, Carl M. Hubbard, and Daniel T. Walz, available at http://bobsfiles.home.att.net/trinity .htm.

Chapter 2: When Conservative Is Risky

The difficulty of fashioning an income-only portfolio with stocks is explored in "Retirement Income Redesigned: Master Plans for Distribution, an Adviser's Guide for Funding Boomers' Best Year," edited by Harold Evensky and Deena B. Katz (Bloomberg Press, 2006).

The research arm of the Vanguard Group reviewed common retiree spending strategies, pitfalls, and best practices in "Spending from a Portfolio: Implications of a Total-Return Approach Versus an Income Approach for Taxable Investors." See https://institutional.vanguard .com/iip/pdf/wp_totalret.pdf.

Chapter 3: Stocks for the Timid

Gene Fama Jr. wrote an excellent article titled "Bonds for Wealth," which discuses the perils of overreliance on bonds in a portfolio. See www.ifa.com/library/articles/bondsforwealth.pdf.

See also an article titled "Think Total Return" by Bryan Olson, available at the Charles Schwab website (www.schwab.com/public/schwab/

research_strategies/market_insight/investing_strategies/portfolio
_planning/think_total_return.html?cmsid=p-1273682&lvl1=research
_strategies&lvl2=market_insight&refid=P-1052764&refpid=P-1004536).

Part Two: Stocks Made Simple
Chapter 4: Stock Picking Perils

You can find the *Wall Street Journal* article on widows and
stocks (November 10, 2008) at MarketWatch's website (www
.marketwatch.com/news/story/any-stock-safe-long-term/story
.aspx?guid=%7bcf047e79-0b68-471a-8c0b-c50767d2d0ff%7d&dist=
tnmostmailed).

For data on the long-term performance of stocks, see the helpful
charts and related information at www.ifa.com/resilienceofcapital
ism.asp.

For a chart listing well-known companies that filed for bankruptcy,
see Table 3-2 at www.ifa.com/12steps/step3/step3page2.asp.

Chapter 5: Balancing Risk and Returns

On December 9, 2008, interest rates on four-week Treasury bills fell
to 0 percent. See www.usatoday.com/money/perfi/bonds/2008-12-09
-treasury-bills-zero-interest_n.htm?csp=23&rm_exclude=aol.

The historical figures come from Ibbotson Associates. See http://
corporate.morningstar.com/ib/asp/subject.aspx?xmlfile=1383
.xml&ad=07cat. They aren't available to the general public.

You can find more information on the Vanguard funds in my
recommended portfolios by going to the fund page on Vanguard's
website (www.vanguard.com). I have no affiliation with Vanguard.

Chapter 6: High Fund Expenses Are Your Mortal Enemy

For a helpful article demonstrating the negative effect of high costs
on investor's returns, see https://personal.vanguard.com/jumppage/
simplestrategies.

For a damning indictment of active investment management, read the May 2008 interview with Kenneth R. French—a professor of finance at Dartmouth College, a consultant to Dimensional Fund Advisors (DFA), and the author of countless investing articles. See www .advisorperspectives.com/pdfs/our_interview_with_ken_french .pdf.

In his most recent study, "The Cost of Active Investing," French estimates that between 1980 and 2006, the average investor lost sixty-seven basis points (0.67 percent) by foregoing indexing. In 2006, that lost cost was $101.6 billion and possibly more.

Chapter 7: The Investing Secret Your Broker Won't Tell You

I set forth the overwhelming data supporting indexing in *The Smartest Investment Book You'll Ever Read* (Perigee Books, 2006).

For an in-depth discussion of the tax efficiency of index funds and the Bogle study, see www.ifa.com/12steps/step7/step7page2.asp.

Attorney and author W. Scott Simon wrote an excellent six-part series for *Morningstar Advisor* on the benefits of indexing. See www .advisor.morningstar.com/articles/articlelist.asp?colId=536.

A depository of hundreds of articles on indexing and model investing can be found on the website of Index Funds Advisors, with whom I'm affiliated (www.ifa.com).

Chapter 8: Make a Date with Target-Date Funds

For a helpful (and exhaustive) overview of target-date funds, see https://institutional.vanguard.com/iip/pdf/ICR4KC.pdf.

Read the *Wall Street Journal*'s "Target-Date Funds Shake Up the Mix," from December 21, 2007, for an overview of problems with some of these all-in-one funds; available at www.filife.com/stories/targetdate -funds-shake-up-the-mix.

A July 3, 2008, piece in *Business Week*, "Target-Date Funds Hit Their Stride," discusses improvements in target-date funds. See

www.businessweek.com/magazine/content/08_28/b4092054950813
.htm?chan=magazine+channel_special+report.

Chapter 9: Resist the Allure of ETFs

For a comparison of ETFs with low-cost index funds, see these articles: www.altruistfa.com/etfs.htm and www.efficientfrontier .com/ef/901/shootout.htm.

To keep abreast of the latest exchange-traded fund news, go to www.IndexUniverse.com.

Morningstar is a depository for ETF statistics, information, and trends (www.morningstar.com/Cover/ETF.html).

Dan Culloton, an analyst with fund tracker Morningstar, is quoted expressing his concerns about investing in ETFs in an article available at www.washingtonpost.com/wp-dyn/articles/A20447 -2005Apr2.html. Culloton concluded:

> I think sector ETFs are a very dangerous and potentially very expensive toy that most people could do without.... If the average professional money manager can't beat the market, what are the chances of the average individual investor beating the market? The best way to capture gross returns, as much as you can, is to buy a broad-based fund and hang onto it forever. Buy and hold is boring, but it's effective in the long run.

Part Three: Bonds Made Simple

Chapter 10: Bonds in a Nutshell

A comprehensive place to research bond funds and check returns, as well as expense ratios, is www.morningstar.com.

You can find a good tutorial on bond basics at www.investopedia .com/university/bonds.

If you want to learn more about fixed-income investing, there are very few books devoted to bonds. A notable exception is *The Only Guide to a Winning Bond Strategy You'll Ever Need: The Way Smart Money*

Preserves Wealth Today (Truman Talley Books, 2006), by Larry Swedroe and Joseph H. Hempen.

Chapter 11: Blindsided by Bonds

Here is an account from Morningstar about the short-term bond fiasco: http://news.morningstar.com/articlenet/article.aspx?id=251658&_QSBPA=Y.

The Schwab fund was recently revived. A Morningstar analyst called Schwab YieldPlus an "unmitigated disaster."

For a press release about the arbitrations filed relating to this fund, see http://biz.yahoo.com/pz/081006/151651.html.

Chapter 12: Avoid Treasury Inflation–Protected Securities

You can find Daily Treasury Yield Curve Rates at www.treas.gov/offices/domestic-finance/debt-management/interest-rate/yield.shtml; you can find Daily Treasury Real (TIPS) Yield Curve Rates at www.treas.gov/offices/domestic-finance/debt-management/interest-rate/real_yield.shtml. You can also find the yields each day in the *Wall Street Journal* and on www.bloomberg.com.

You can find a helpful article on TIPS at http://news.morningstar.com/articlenet/article.aspx?id=82054&_QSBPA=Y.

See an article titled "TIPS Prove Poor Tip for Traders Betting on Inflation," available at http://bloomberg.com/apps/news?pid=20601009&sid=agxFn.wFZrlc&refer=bond.

Part Four: Cash Made Simple
Chapter 13: You Need Cash Insurance

The Federal Deposit Insurance Corp. maintains a great deal of information on FDIC coverage of bank deposits. See www.fdic.gov/quicklinks/consumers.html.

To calculate your FDIC insurance coverage for each of your bank

accounts, consult EDIE the Estimator at www2.fdic.gov/edie/index
.html.

For the FDIC's list of failed banks as well as the dates they closed,
see www.fdic.gov/bank/individual/failed/banklist.html.

For an Associated Press story on the number of bank failures, see
www.usatoday.com/money/industries/banking/2008-11-25-fdic
-problem-banks_n.htm.

Chapter 14: The Holy Grail: More Reward, Same Risk

"The Fine Print: 10 Secrets Your Bank Keeps" by Jim Rendon at
SmartMoney Magazine (July 20, 2008) discusses the reality of the biggest banks being stingy with their customers. See www.msnbc.msn
.com/id/25736566/print/1/displaymode/1098.

For a helpful article on smaller banks paying higher interest rates, see
www.helium.com/items/82583-which-bank-pays-the-highest-interest
-rate-on-savings.

Wikipedia has an excellent overview of certificates of deposit. See
http://en.wikipedia.org/wiki/Certificate_of_deposit.

Chapter 15: Money Market Funds Make Money

For a *New York Times* article about the Reserve Fund's financial diffi-
culties, see www.nytimes.com/2008/10/29/business/29fund.html?_r
=1&pagewanted=print.

Here's a *USA Today* story on the Reserve Fund's problems: www
.usatoday.com/money/perfi/funds/2008-11-10-reserve-primary
-money-market-fund_N.htm.

For a *MarketWatch* story that mentions the historic breaking of the
buck by Community Bankers U.S. Government Money Fund in 1994,
see www.marketwatch.com/news/story/story.aspx?guid={d565e50b
-ef4d-45e8-be27-71bf33c7b1b0}.

Here's the press release from the U.S. Department of the Treasury

on the temporary money market insurance coverage: www.treasury
.gov/press/releases/hp1147.htm.

For an overview of money market funds, see http://banking.about
.com/od/investments/a/moneymarketfund.htm.

Part Five: Annuities Made Simple

Chapter 16: Immediately Consider Immediate Annuities

The TIAA-CREF study on the utility of immediate annuities, "Making Retirement Income Last a Lifetime," was published by the *Journal of Financial Planning* in its December 2001 issue. The landmark study suggested that immediate annuities can decrease the chances that a retiree will die impoverished. See www.ibmemployee.com/pdfs/makingretirementlast.pdf. Here is another helpful article that deals with many of the concerns investors have with immediate annuities: www.insurancenewsnet.com/article.asp?a=top_lh&id=87015.

From its Plain Talk Library series, Vanguard published a twelve-page booklet titled *Should You Consider an Income Annuity?* that addresses questions about immediate annuities. See www.vanguard.com/pdf/ptia.pdf.

For an excellent study by Milliman Inc. titled "Immediate Annuities and Retirement Income Portfolios," demonstrating the value of adding an immediate annuity to your retirement nest egg, see www.milliman.com/expertise/life-financial/publications/rr/pdfs/immediate-annuities-retirement-income-rr05-19-08.pdf.

Here's an article making the case for *not* investing in inflation-protected immediate annuities: www.insurancenewsnet.com/article
.asp?a=sa&neID=20060703376.1_2af50038a33797ac.

Chapter 17: The Annuity That Keeps on Giving

To learn about charitable gift annuities and current recommended rates, visit the website of the American Council on Gift Annuities at www.acga-web.org.

The New York State Insurance Department published a helpful list of the top ten questions about charitable gift annuities. See www.ins .state.ny.us/que_top10/que_life_cha.htm.

Fidelity Investments published an excellent report on the benefit of giving appreciated stocks and mutual funds through charitable donations. See http://personal.fidelity.com/myfidelity/insidefidelity/ newscenter/mediadocs/smart_giving_report.pdf. The report concludes that ten to twenty million American households have the potential to realize additional tax savings by donating securities with long-term appreciation to charity or to a donor-advised fund instead of contributing cash directly to charities. In short, millions could save billions or give billions more instead.

Chapter 18: Just Say No to Variable Annuities

For more on why the financial press and fee-only planners are extremely leery of variable annuities, read the U.S. Securities and Exchange Commission's consumer warning "Variable Annuities: What You Should Know" at www.sec.gov/investor/pubs/varannty .htm.

Craig J. McCann and Kaye A. Thomas wrote a particularly damning article about the problems with variable annuities. You can find it at http://slcg.com/pdf/workingpapers/annuities.pdf.

Chapter 19: The Inequitable Annuity

For a compelling indictment of the equity-indexed annuity industry, read "An Economic Analysis of Equity-Indexed Annuities" by Craig J. McCann, of the Securities Litigation & Consulting Group Inc., at http://slcg.com/pdf/workingpapers/eia%20white%20paper .pdf. McCann reached this chilling conclusion: "Unsophisticated investors will continue to be victimized by issuers of equity-indexed annuities until truthful disclosure and the absence of sales practice abuses is assured."

The SEC recently approved a new rule "to help protect seniors and other investors from fraudulent and abusive practices that can occur in the sale of equity-indexed annuities." See the press release at http://sec.gov/news/press/2008/2008-298.htm.

Part Six: Mining Your Money
Chapter 20: Undermining Your Money
For an article discussing Peter Lynch's flawed withdrawal advice, see www.retirement-financial-advisor.com/run_out.htm.

To learn more about the T. Rowe Price study, read the *Medical Economics* story "Will You Outlive Your Nest Egg," dated March 9, 2003, at http://medicaleconomics.modernmedicine.com/memag/modern medicine+now/will-you-outlive-your-nest-egg/articlestandard/article/detail/112450.

Chapter 21: The 4 Percent Rule
William Bernstein wrote an excellent series of articles titled "The Retirement Calculator from Hell." You can access them at www.efficientfrontier.com/ef/998/hell.htm.

William P. Bengen, a certified financial planner in El Cajon, California, is largely responsible for the widespread use of the 4 percent withdrawal rate in retirement. Beginning in the mid-1990s, Bengen wrote a series of landmark papers on safe withdrawal rates. His aim was to pinpoint withdrawal strategies that would provide investors with near certainty that they wouldn't outlast their nest egg for at least thirty years. Bengen settled on a conservative withdrawal rate that would have kept the nest egg alive during the bear markets of the Great Depression and World War II and during the 1970s. Although his original study didn't cover the infamous dot-com bust of the early 2000s, he later determined that it would have survived that too.

In the accompanying chart, you'll see how destructive these four bear markets were for owners of blue chip stocks, which are considered the sturdiest stocks you can buy.

FOUR MAJOR BEAR MARKETS SINCE THE 1920S (LARGE-CAP STOCKS)

Period	Duration (Months)	Total Return (Percent)
September 1929–February 1933	42	−77.7
March 1937–March 1938	13	−50.0
January 1973–December 1974	24	−37.3
September 2000–September 2002	25	−44.2

Bengen also examined the impact inflation had on retiree portfolios during these bear markets as well as during the other historical periods in his studies. Of the four major bear markets, the one that hurt retirees the most would have been the one that struck in the 1970s. Why? Because of raging inflation.

Here are Bengen's papers, which appeared in the *Journal of Financial Planning*:

"Determining Withdrawal Rates Using Historical Data," January 1994, available at www.bobneiman.com/NWM_Pages/Determining%20Withdrawal%20Rates%20-%20William%20Bengen.pdf.
"Conserving Client Retirement, Part III," *Journal of Financial Planning*, December 1997, pp. 84–97.

Here are two other influential withdrawal studies, written by Jonathan T. Guyton and published in the *Journal of Financial Planning*:

"Decision Rules and Maximum Initial Withdrawal Rates," March 2006, available at www.bobneiman.com/NWM_Pages/Decision%20Rules%20&%20Maximum%20Initial%20Withdrawal%20Rates%20-%20Guyton%202006.pdf.
"Decision Rules and Portfolio Management for Retirees: Is the 'Safe' Initial Withdrawal Rate Too Safe?" October 2004, available

at www.bobneiman.com/NWM_Pages/Decision%20Rules%20&
%20Portfolio%20Management%20for%20Retirees%20Safe
%20Withdrawal%20Rate%20-%20John%20Guyton.pdf.

Chapter 22: Squeezing Your Nest Egg Hard

Here is William P. Bengen's table of peak withdrawals for a portfolio that contains intermediate government bonds and large- and
small-cap stocks.

Time Horizon (Years)	Peak Withdrawal Rate (Percent)	Total Equity Allocation (Percent)
10	8.9	40
15	6.3	30
20	5.2	30
25	4.7	45
30	4.4	50
35	4.3	60
40	4.2	65

For an excellent article on the 4 percent rule and the role of inflation, see "Retirement: The 4 Percent Solution," by financial columnist
Walter Updegrave, at http://money.cnn.com/2007/08/13/pf/expert/
expert.moneymag/index.htm?postversion=2007081410.

Chapter 23: Squeezing Your Nest Egg Harder

Michael Kitces—the director of financial planning for Pinnacle
Advisory Group, a wealth management firm in Columbia, Maryland—
released a lengthy report in May 2008 titled "Resolving the Paradox—
Is the Safe Withdrawal Rate Sometimes Too Safe?" See www.kitces
.com/assets/pdfs/Kitces_Report_May_2008.pdf.

For an article discussing Kitces's work, see www.onwallstreet.com/
asset/article/613331/market-based-withdrawals.html?pg=.

Chapter 24: Squeezing Your Nest Egg Hardest

William P. Bengen reviewed his past research and discussed his latest views on safe nest egg withdrawal rates in his book *Conserving Client Portfolios During Retirement* (Financial Planning Association, 2006).

For a discussion of Bengen's floor-to-ceiling approach and other withdrawal strategies, see http://bobsfiles.home.att.net/Variable Withdrawals.html#bengen.

You can find Bengen's article "Conserving Client Portfolios During Retirement, Part IV" at http://bobsfiles.home.att.net/pdfs/ Conserving_Client_Portfolios_During_Retirement_Part_IV.pdf.

Part Seven: Simple Steps to Stretch Your Money

Chapter 25: Basic Withdrawal Strategies

The figures for the dramatic fates of two $1.4 million nest eggs were obtained during in an interview by Lynn O'Shaughnessy with James Lange—CPA, estate attorney, and author of *Retire Secure! Pay Taxes Later: The Key to Making Your Money Last As Long As You Do*, 2nd edition.

To learn more about tax withdrawal strategies, see this report from the TIAA-CREF Institute by William Reichenstein—a Baylor University professor, an associate editor of the *Journal of Investing*, and a member of the editorial board of the *Journal of Financial Education*: "Tax-Efficient Sequencing of Accounts to Tap in Retirement," available at www.tiaa -crefinstitute.org/articles/tr100106.html.

For information about the tax rules governing inherited Roth IRAs, see www.fairmark.com/rothira/inherit.htm.

Chapter 26: Moving Your Retirement Accounts

For an excellent series of articles on 401(k) rollover options, see www .bankrate.com/brm/news/financial_literacy/retirement_investing/ IRA_rollover_a1.asp.

Chapter 27: Roth Redux

CPA and estate planning attorney James Lange has written many articles about Roth IRAs and their considerable advantages. For more information about Roth conversion opportunities provided by the Tax Increase Prevention and Reconciliation Act, see his article at www.rothira-advisor.com/roth_ira_conversion_and_new_tax_cut.htm.

CCH issued a special report on this act and included a helpful section on the new rules governing Roth conversions. See http://tax.cch group.com/Legislation/TIPRA.pdf.

To avoid an IRA tax disaster, you may need expert advice. You'll want to rely on a certified public accountant, an estate attorney, or an investment advisor who is a true expert on IRA rules.

You can assess a professional's abilities by the resource materials he uses, including any of the following: *Ed Slott's IRA Advisor* newsletter; Leimberg Information Services Inc.; *Life and Death Planning for Retirement Benefits,* by Natalie Choate; and Brentmark Software's Retirement Plan Analyzer.

To learn more about the care and handling of IRAs, pick up a copy of Slott's *Your Complete Retirement Planning Road Map: A Comprehensive Action Plan for Securing IRAs, 401(k)s, and Other Retirement Plans for Yourself and Your Family* (Ballantine Books, 2007), which contains numerous handy checklists to keep IRA owners from making costly mistakes.

Chapter 28: The Reverse Holdup: Required Distribution Rules

An excellent resource for mandatory retirement withdrawal information is Natalie Choate's *Life and Death Planning for Retirement Benefits: The Essential Handbook for Estate Planners,* 6th edition (Ataxplan Publications, 2006).

For an article on recent legislation by Congress eliminating minimum distributions for 2009, see http://webcpa.com/article.cfm?articleid=30199&pg=ros.

Part Eight: Social Security and Pensions: Critical Choices
Chapter 29: Winning the Social Security Lottery
Your birth date will dictate when you'll qualify for full Social Security benefits. The age breakdown is shown in the accompanying chart:

Year of Birth	Full Retirement Age
1937 or earlier	65
1938	65 years 2 months
1939	65 years 4 months
1940	65 years 6 months
1941	65 years 8 months
1942	65 years 10 months
1943–1954	66 years
1955	66 years 2 months
1956	66 years 4 months
1957	66 years 6 months
1958	66 years 8 months
1959	66 years 10 months
1960 and later	67

Glenn S. Daily's "Delaying Social Security Benefits: A Real Options Perspective" provides good information on the timing of Social Security payments. See http://glenndaily.com/socialsecurity.htm.

The website of the Social Security Administration contains a wealth of data about Social Security benefits (www.ssa.gov).

Chapter 30: Leaving Your Spouse a Legacy of Poverty
For information about women and Social Security, visit www.socialsecurity.gov/women.

The study on women and Social Security is "Why Do Women Claim

Social Security Benefits So Early?" by Alicia H. Munnell and Mauricio Soto of the Center for Retirement Research at Boston College. You can access it at http://crr.bc.edu/images/stories/Briefs/ib_35.pdf?phpMy Admin=43ac483c4de9t51d9eb41.

The center also produced another pertinent study in October 2007: "Why Do Married Men Claim Social Security Benefits So Early? Ignorance or Caddishness?" You can access it at http://crr.bc.edu/images/stories/Working_Papers/wp_2007-17.pdf?phpMyAdmin=43ac483c4d e9t51d9eb41.

With Nadia Karamcheva, Munnell also wrote the article "Why Are Widows So Poor?" Among the reasons they note is the drop in Social Security and pension benefits. You can access it at http://crr.bc.edu/briefs/why_are_widows_so_poor.html.

Chapter 31: Leaning on a Thin (Pension) Reed

To read about how financial giants covet the management of pension assets, see Matthew Goldstein's August 8, 2008, *Business Week* story at www.businessweek.com/magazine/content/08_33/b4096000769608 .htm.

For an excellent academic article that explains how cash benefit plans penalize older workers with more seniority, see "Cash Balance Plans," by Graham R. Mitenko, Michael J. O'Hara, and Gerald V. Boyles, available at http://cba.unomaha.edu/faculty/mohara/web/ CBPP-INET.html.

For a sobering look at the present and future problems of the nation's pension plans, both private and public, read financial journalist Roger Lownstein's *While America Aged: How Pension Debts Ruined General Motors, Stopped the NYC Subways, Bankrupted San Diego, and Loom as the Next Financial Crisis* (Penguin Press, 2008).

You'll learn what employers have been doing recently to change their pension plans in this October 2007 Vanguard report: "Recent

Changes to Defined Benefit Plan Design: 2000–2006," available at http://institutional.vanguard.com/VGApp/iip/site/institutional/researchcommentary/article?File=ChgsToDBPlan2000_2006.

Chapter 32: Pension Distribution Elections Are Critical

Check out "Effects of the Pension Protection Act of 2006 on Lump Sum 401k Distributions" at http://research401k.com/pension-payout .html.

To learn more about why women face financial perils in retirement, read "Why Are Widows So Poor?" by Nadia Karamcheva and Alicia H. Munnell at Boston College's Center for Retirement Research. See http://crr.bc.edu/briefs/why_are_widows_so_poor_.html.

AARP issued a detailed study titled "Pension Lump-Sum Distributions: Do Boomers Take Them or Save Them?" available at http://assets.aarp.org/rgcenter/econ/dd144_pension.pdf.

Part Nine: Is Sixty-Five the New Fifty?

Chapter 34: Retirement Delayed Is Retirement Enhanced

In 2004, the Congressional Budget Office reviewed the past decade's research on the retirement prospects of aging Americans. Its "Retirement Age and the Need for Saving" concluded that a substantial number of baby boomers wouldn't be able to maintain their current consumption levels if they didn't push back their retirement date; available at http://cbo.gov/doc.cfm?index=5419&type=0.

For an excellent article, "Optimizing Your Retirement Income: What Works Best and Why," by Christine Fahlund, see http://investor .financialcounsel.com/Articles/RetirementPlanning/ARTRET 0000050-OptimizingYourRetirementIncome.pdf. Fahlund concludes: "Generally, no single decision will improve pre-retirees' potential retirement security as much as continuing to work even a few more years beyond the anticipated retirement date."

**Chapter 36: Don't Count on Age Discrimination Laws
to Protect Your Job**

For more about the number of aging Americans in the workforce,
see "Trends in Labor Force Participation in the United States" in the
U.S. Bureau of Labor Statistic's *Monthly Labor Review,* October 2006.

The U.S. Equal Employment Opportunity Commission has a copy
of the landmark Age Discrimination in Employment Act of 1967
(ADEA) at http://eeoc.gov/policy/adea.html.

For a history of ADEA and how the act affects employees today,
see "How Do Age Discrimination Laws Affect Older Workers?"
by Joanna N. Lahey, a research associate at the Center for Retirement Research at Boston College. See http://crr.bc.edu/index
.php?option=com_content&task=emailform&id=98.

AARP published a helpful study for employers titled "Age Discrimination: What Employers Need to Know." The information in
the study is useful for employees as well. See http://assets.aarp.org/
www.aarp.org_/articles/money/employers/age_discrimination.pdf.

Chapter 37: Part-Time Work Can Be Full-Time Trouble

The Merrill Lynch study titled "The 2006 Merrill Lynch New Retirement Study" can be found at www.ml.com/media/66482.pdf.

Part Ten: Financial Lifelines for Desperate Times

Chapter 38: The Reverse Mortgage Wheel of Fortune

For statistics on reverse mortgages, go to the National Reverse Mortgage Lenders Association at http://nrmlaonline.org/rms/statistics/
default.aspx?article_id=601.

Chapter 39: Reverse Mortgages: Too Good to Be True?

For an excellent discussion of reverse mortgages, including a
summary of the new federal housing law raising the ceiling on the

amount seniors can borrow, see www.bankrate.com/bos/news/
retirementguide2008/20081103-reverse-mortgages-a1.asp?caret=3c.

Chapter 40: Making Usury Look Good: The Real Costs of Reverse Mortgages

For a particularly gripping example of how reverse mortgage
fees can turn into serious financial disasters, read the testimony
from the U.S. Senate Special Committee on Aging's December 17,
2007, hearing, available at http://aging.senate.gov/minority/index
.cfm?Fuseaction=Hearings.Detail&HearingID=9a59e516-2933-4c2e
-b91d-bb01336bd016.

The new national regulations cap the origination fees for these loans.
Lenders can charge up to 2 percent of the loan amount for the first
$200,000 of the value of the home and 1 percent on the balance. There
is an overall cap of $6,000. For an article discussing the new rules and
regulations for reverse mortgages, see www.affil.org/media2/lending
-in-the-news/lending-in-the-news/reverse-mortgages-retooled.

Bankrate, a very reliable source of financial information, published a
series of articles on the new rules. See www.bankrate.com/yho/news/
retirementguide2008/20081103-reverse-mortgages-a1.asp?caret=3c.

AARP issued an exhaustive report on the pluses and minuses
of reverse mortgages, available at http://assets.aarp.org/rgcenter/
consume/2007_22_revmortgage.pdf.

Chapter 41: Low-Cost Lifelines

For an article listing various sources of financial help for seniors, see
www.suntimes.com/business/currency/1319447,senior-help-programs
-120808.article.

Chapter 42: Should You Sell Your Life?

Learn about the hazards of life settlements in a FINRA Investor Alert titled "Seniors Beware: What You Should Know About Life

Settlements," available at www.finra.org/Investors/ProtectYourself/
InvestorAlerts/AnnuitiesAndInsurance/P018469.

For a nicely balanced series of articles about life settlements, see
www.bankrate.com/brm/news/insurance/life-settlements-a1.asp.

Chapter 43: Help When It Seems Hopeless

The statistics on the number of eligible seniors who don't apply
for food stamps came from a July 2, 2008, *USA Today* article by Lynn
O'Shaughnessy, available at www.usatoday.com/money/perfi/
retirement/2008-07-01-retiree-fixed-income_N.htm.

Part Eleven: Care Costs

Chapter 44: Care Before Medicare

The statistics on employers offering retiree healthcare were gath-
ered for the Henry J. Kaiser Family Foundation's Employer Health
Benefits 2008 Annual Survey, available at http://ehbs.kff.org.

To learn more about health insurance, check out the National Health
Law Program's www.healthcarecoach.com.

For more about HIPAA, go to the U.S. Department of Labor's
Employee Benefits Security Administration at www.dol.gov/ebsa/
faqs/faq_consumer_hipaa.html.

For more information about COBRA, see the frequently asked questions published on the Department of Labor's website (www.dol.gov/
ebsa/faqs/faq_consumer_cobra.html).

Chapter 45: The Short Skinny on Long-Term Care

You can find statistics on the cost of long-term care at the U.S.
Department of Health and Human Services' National Clearinghouse
for Long-Term Care Information (www.longtermcare.gov/LTC/
Main_Site/Paying_LTC/Costs_Of_Care/Costs_Of_Care.aspx).

Chapter 46: Who Needs Long-Term Care Insurance?

Elder Law Answers covers many of the key issues about long-term care insurance, including how much coverage is needed and what features are important. See http://elderlawanswers.com/elder_info/elder_article.asp?id=2595.

The U.S. Department of Health and Human Services has an excellent website discussing long-term care policies and Medicare. See www.medicare.gov/longtermcare/static/home.asp.

For a discussion of long-term care insurance, including the factors to consider if you are contemplating its purchase, see www.bankrate.com/brm/news/retirementguide2008/20081103-health-insurance-costs-a3.asp?caret=1b.

Consumer Reports has a fine article on long-term care coverage. See www.consumerreports.org/cro/money/insurance/longterm-care-insurance-1103/overview/.

Chapter 47: When Fat Beats Skinny: Choosing the Right Long-Term Care Insurance

Michael Kitces, Pinnacle Advisory Group's director of financial planning, wrote "Developing Financial Planner Recommendations for Long-Term Care Insurance Policies" (June 2008). See www.kitces.com (access requires a subscription).

For the perspective of the health insurance industry on this issue, see an article titled "Shelton Surveys the Changing LTC Insurance Scene," available at www.nahu.org/meetings/annual/2006/ShowDaily Monday.pdf.

Chapter 48: Keeping Your Long-Term Care Policy in Force

To find the premium costs for long-term care coverage, see www.longtermcare.gov/LTC/Main_Site/Paying_LTC/Private_Programs/LTC_Insurance/index.aspx.

For the June 26, 2008, Fidelity Investments survey, see www.reuters
.com/article/pressRelease/idUS126278+26-Jun-2008+BW20080626.

For a discussion of the Fidelity survey concerning yearly premiums seniors will pay for joint long-term care over their lifetimes, see
www.insurancenewsnet.com/article.asp?n=1&innID=20080626290
.2_de7f0342dff0fac7.

For AARP's overall views on long-term care coverage and the various policy options available to purchasers, see www.aarp.org/money/
financial_planning/sessionfive/longterm_care_insurance.html.

Chapter 49: Where's the Check? Making Claims and Getting Paid

The *New York Times* story about the long-term care industry ran on
March 26, 2007, and is available at www.nytimes.com/2007/03/26/
business/26care.html?scp=2&sq=%22long+term+care+insurance%
22+and+%22lawsuits%22&st=nyt.

The *Times* ran follow-up stories focused on congressional inves-
tigations of the long-term care industry, including a May 25, 2007,
piece available at www.nytimes.com/2007/05/25/business/25care
.html?scp=1&sq=congress+putting+long-term+care+under+
scrutiny&st=nyt. A *Times* story from October 3, 2007, is available at
www.nytimes.com/2007/10/03/business/03care.html?scp=1&sq=
scrutiny+for+insurers+of+the+aged&st=nyt.

Part Twelve: The State of Your Estate
Chapter 50: Find the Will to Leave a Will

To learn more about estate planning, go to www.nolo.com. Nolo
also publishes many books geared toward consumers on issues
surrounding estate planning.

For an example of why it's crucial to change your beneficiary forms
when your life circumstances change, read a story titled "Beneficiary
Documentation Case Goes to High Court," available at www.investment
news.com.

Chapter 51: Avoiding Probate Purgatory

The State Bar of California has an excellent series of articles on living trusts. See www.calbar.ca.gov/state/calbar/calbar_generic.jsp ?cid=10581&id=2212.

For more information about payable-on-death and joint accounts, see http://wills.about.com/od/howtoavoidprobate/a/jointpod.htm.

For information on the Uniform Transfer-on-Death Security Registration Act, including a summary of its provisions, see www.nccusl .org/nccusl/uniformact_summaries/uniformacts-s-tutsra.asp.

Chapter 52: The Magic Power of an Inherited IRA

The figures for this chapter were obtained from an interview by Lynn O'Shaughnessy with one of the nation's leading experts on IRAs, Ed Slott, CPA.

For an overview of your options when you are fortunate enough to inherit an IRA, see http://personal.fidelity.com/products/retirement/ inheritedira/parentorother.shtml.

Chapter 53: Irrevocable Trusts Require Trust

You can find a summary of the differences between revocable and irrevocable trusts at www.taxprophet.com/pubs/trust_nl.html.

The National Conference of Commissioners on Uniform State Laws developed the Prudent Investor Act based on the Prudent Investor Rule. You can find out more about the landmark act by visiting the NCCUSL's website (www.nccusl.org).

Chapter 54: I Love You, but Let's Sign on the Dotted Line: Prenups for Seniors

The authoritative guide on prenuptial agreements is *Prenuptial Agreements: How to Write a Fair and Lasting Contract*, by Katherine E. Stoner and Shae Irving (Nolo, October 2008).

The Ohio Department of Aging published a thoughtful article on the need for prenuptial agreements "the second time around," available at http://ohioline.osu.edu/ss-fact/pdf/0184.pdf.old.

Part Thirteen: Wolves in Sheep's Clothing
Chapter 55: Mail-Order Experts

The North American Securities Administrators Association's investor alert on so-called senior specialists can be found at http://nasaa.org/Investor_Education/Investor_Alerts___Tips/7181.cfm.

The U.S. Securities and Exchange Commission weighs in on senior specialists at http://sec.gov/investor/pubs/senior-profdes.htm.

The *New York Times* story "For Elderly Investors, Instant Experts Abound" can be found at http://query.nytimes.com/gst/fullpage.html?res=9507EFD8133EF93BA35754C0A9619C8B63&sec=&spon=&pagewanted=all.

Chapter 56: Expensive Free Meals

A yearlong examination of free lunch investment seminars, conducted by state and federal regulators, determined that 100 percent of the seminars were sales presentations. About 50 percent of the seminars sponsored by securities firms featured exaggerated or misleading advertising claims. The report, titled "Protecting Senior Investors: Report of Examinations of Securities Firms Providing 'Free Lunch' Sales Seminars," was the culmination of an effort by the SEC, North American Securities Administrators Association, and FINRA. See http://sec.gov/spotlight/seniors/freelunchreport.pdf.

FINRA has an investor alert posted on its website that discusses the many ways unethical pitchmen try to convince soon-to-be retirees to cash in their retirement savings. See http://finra.org/Investors/ProtectYourself/InvestorAlerts/RetirementAccounts/p017365.

Chapter 57: Whom Can You Trust?

For W. Scott Simon's excellent *Morningstar Advisor* Fiduciary Focus columns, go to www.advisor.morningstar.com/articles/articlelist .asp?colId=536.

You can learn more about the importance of retaining the services of a fiduciary investment advisor at the website of the National Association of Personal Financial Advisors (www.napfa.org).

The Bernard Madoff Ponzi scheme caused many to wonder why the manner in which he conducted business did not raise red flags for regulators and investors. For a particularly thoughtful commentary, see the article by John C. Coffee Jr., professor of law at Columbia University Law School and director of its Center on Corporate Governance, available at www.cnn.com/2008/POLITICS/12/16/coffee .madoff/index.html.

APPENDIX A

Asset Allocation

This questionnaire will help guide you to a proper asset allocation for your retirement portfolio. This is meant only as a guide. For each individual investor, there are many factors that cannot possibly be addressed in a generic questionnaire. You may also wish to take this questionnaire online at www.smartestinvestmentbook.com.

Step 1: Add up all of the money that you currently have saved for retirement. This should include 401(k) plans, 403(b) plans, and all IRAs you are using to save for retirement. Write this number down here:

Current Retirement Savings _____   ....A

Step 2: What are your annual living expenses?

Annual Living Expenses _____   ....B

Step 3: At what annual rate (in percent) do you expect your salary to grow for the foreseeable future?

Annual Salary Growth Rate _____ C

Step 4: How much are you contributing (in dollars) to retirement plans? Include your contributions to all retirement plans and include any matching contributions from your employer.

Annual Retirement Contributions _____   ....D

Step 5: Ratio of Current Retirement Savings to Annual Living Expenses. Divide the figure in Step 1 by the figure in Step 2. For example, if you have $250,000 currently saved for retirement and your living expenses are $50,000, this ratio would be 5.

$$\frac{\text{Current Retirement Savings (A)}}{\text{Annual Living Expenses (B)}} = \underline{\hspace{3cm}}$$

Step 6: Figure out how many years you have until retirement. For example, if you are fifty-five and plan to retire at seventy, you have fifteen years until retirement.

Years Until Retirement = _____

Step 7: SAS. In the matrix below, find the intersection of your years until retirement (found in the far left column) and your ratio of current retirement savings to annual living expenses (found across the top). Identify the number in this cell. This is your savings-age score (SAS). To continue the example, if your ratio of current retirement savings to annual living expenses is 5 and you plan to retire in fifteen years, your SAS is 30.

SAS SCORE = _____

How many years before retirement?	Ratio of current retirement savings to annual living expenses											
	<1	1–2	2–4	4–6	6–8	8–10	10–12	12–14	14–16	16–18	18–20	>20
41 to 45 years	80	78	72	60	40	28	20	12	8	4	2	0
36 to 40 years	76	74	68	57	38	27	19	11	8	4	2	0
31 to 35 years	72	71	65	54	36	25	18	11	7	4	1	0
26 to 30 years	68	67	61	51	34	24	17	10	7	3	1	0
21 to 25 years	56	55	50	42	28	20	14	8	6	3	1	0
16 to 20 years	48	47	43	36	24	17	12	7	5	2	1	0
11 to 15 years	40	39	36	30	20	14	10	6	4	2	1	0
6 to 10 years	24	24	22	18	12	8	6	4	2	1	0	0
1 to 5 years	16	16	14	12	8	6	4	2	2	1	0	0
Retired	8	8	7	6	4	3	2	1	1	0	0	0

Step 8: Ratio of Annual Retirement Contributions to Annual Living Expenses. Divide the figure in Step 4 by the figure in Step 2. For example, if you contribute $5,000 per year to IRAs and your 401(k) (the $5,000 includes your employer's matching contributions) and your annual living expenses are $50,000, this number is 10 percent.

$$\frac{\text{Annual Retirement Contributions (D)}}{\text{Annual Living Expenses (B)}} = \underline{\hspace{2in}}$$

Step 9: GCS. In the matrix below, find the intersection of your annual salary growth rate from Step 3 (found in the far left column) and your ratio of annual retirement contributions to annual living expenses (found across the top). Identify the number in this cell. This is your growth-contribution score (GCS).

GCS SCORE = _____

Annual growth of current salary	Ratio of annual retirement contributions to annual living expenses								
	0%	1–3%	3–5%	5–8%	8–10%	10–15%	15–20%	20–25%	>25%
8%+	15	15	14	11	8	5	4	2	2
5%–8%	14	14	13	11	7	5	4	2	1
3%–5%	14	13	12	10	7	5	3	2	1
1%–3%	13	12	11	10	6	4	3	2	1
0%–1%	11	10	9	8	5	4	3	2	1
0%	9	9	8	7	5	3	2	1	1

Step 10: RAS. Answer the following ten questions. Next to each answer for every question, there is a number in parentheses. When you decide which answer is right for you, make note of the number next to the answer. Once you have finished all of the questions, you will add up these numbers. All of these numbers added together will give you your RAS.

1. *What is your estimate of how your employment income will grow on an annual basis until you retire?*
A. It will remain stable .... (0)
B. It will likely grow by between 1 and 3 percent............................ (1)
C. It will grow by more than 3 but less than 5 percent.................... (2)
D. It will grow by more than 5 but less than 8 percent.................... (3)
E. It will grow by more than 8 percent per year.............................. (4)

2. *How many years have you been investing in the stock market?*
A. None.. (0)
B. Less than 1 year.. (1)
C. More than 1 but less than 5 years .... (2)
D. More than 5 but less than 10 years.. (3)
E. 10 years or more.. (4)

3. *I consider myself to be knowledgeable about investments and financial matters.*
A. Strongly agree .... (4)
B. Agree .... (3)
C. Somewhat agree.. (2)
D. Disagree .... (1)
E. Strongly disagree .... (0)

4. *How do you feel about this statement?*
"I want my investments to be risk free."
(Note: Investments with no risk have little or no expected return beyond the rate of inflation.)
A. Strongly agree .... (0)
B. Agree .... (0)
C. Somewhat agree.. (1)
D. Disagree .... (3)
E. Strongly disagree .... (4)

5. *I am willing to expose my investment portfolio to some degree of risk to increase the likelihood of higher returns.*

A. Strongly agree .... (4)
B. Agree .... (3)
C. Somewhat agree .... (2)
D. Disagree .... (0)
E. Strongly disagree .... (0)

6. *I am comfortable with a portion of my portfolio being invested internationally.*

A. Strongly agree .... (4)
B. Agree .... (3)
C. Somewhat agree .... (2)
D. Disagree .... (1)
E. Strongly disagree .... (0)

7. *When my investment portfolio declines, I begin to think about selling off some of my positions and reinvesting at some later date.*

A. Strongly agree .... (0)
B. Agree .... (1)
C. Somewhat agree .... (2)
D. Disagree .... (3)
E. Strongly disagree .... (4)

8. *Some investors hold portfolios that consist entirely of stocks. Such investors lost approximately 20 percent of their portfolios in October 1987. If you owned a risky investment that fell by 20 percent over a very short period, what would you do?*

A. Sell all the remaining investment .... (0)
B. Sell 75 percent of the remaining investment .... (0)
C. Sell 50 percent of the remaining investment .... (1)
D. Sell 25 percent of the remaining investment .... (2)
E. Hold on to the investment .... (4)

9. *What is the worst twelve-month percentage loss you would toler-
ate for your long-term investments, beyond which you would sell
some or all of your investments?*

A. 42 percent .... (4)

B. 31 percent .... (3)

C. 21 percent .... (2)

D. 10 percent .... (1)

E. 0 percent .... (0)

10. *Based on $100,000 invested since 1975, the following choices show
the highest twelve-month gain and the highest twelve-month loss of
five different index portfolios. Which portfolio would you choose?*
(Note: The portfolios with the widest range between the loss and the gain
also have higher average returns.)

A. Loss of $1,100; gain of $23,500 .... (0)

B. Loss of $11,500; gain of $31,000 .... (1)

C. Loss of $21,800; gain of $42,700 .... (2)

D. Loss of $32,100; gain of $51,600 .... (3)

E. Loss of $42,400; gain of $63,100 .... (4)

RAS SCORE = _____

Step 11: PAS (SAS + GCS + RAS). Add your SAS, your GCS, and
your RAS. This number is your portfolio allocation score (PAS). Find
where your score lies in the distribution on the next page. The matrix
gives you a range for the stock portion of your allocation. Your recommended percentage allocated to stocks in most cases would be in this
range. Once you choose the percent allocation to stocks, the remainder
will be invested in bonds. Of the amount allocated to stocks, remember
that 70 percent of that amount should be in U.S. stocks and 30 percent
of that amount should be in international stocks.

PAS SCORE = _____

| Percent Stocks | | |
PAS	Upper Boundary	Lower Boundary
80–120	90	70
70–79	80	60
60–69	70	50
50–59	60	40
40–49	50	30
30–39	40	20
20–29	30	10
10–19	20	0
0–9	10	0

APPENDIX B

Risk and Return Summaries

The following pages feature three index simulated model portfolios from Vanguard, Fidelity, and T. Rowe Price that show the hypothetical results of four risk levels: low risk (20 percent stocks/80 percent bonds), medium-low risk (40 percent stocks/60 percent bonds), medium-high risk (60 percent stocks/40 percent bonds), and high risk (80 percent stocks/20 percent bonds). In addition, these charts provide the composition of the respective model portfolios and the summary of raw data used to create simulated index performance numbers.

The *average annualized return* (geometric) reflects the performance results of the portfolios referenced.

The *annualized standard deviation* is a statistical measure of the historical volatility of the portfolios referenced.

The data for all portfolios are for the period 1970–2008.

RISK AND RETURN SUMMARY OF
FOUR VANGUARD/INDEX SIMULATED MODEL PORTFOLIOS

Statistic	Portfolio			
	20/80: Low Risk	40/60: Medium-Low Risk	60/40: Medium-High Risk	80/20: High Risk
Average annual return (percent)	8.61	9.08	9.42	9.61
Annualized standard deviation (percent)	6.92	8.85	11.66	14.86
Worst single calendar year (percent)	−3.79	−12.63	−21.47	−30.32
Worst two calendar years (percent)	−0.32	−10.28	−19.74	−28.69
Worst three calendar years (percent)	8.17	−1.21	−15.03	−27.51

CURRENT COMPOSITION OF
FOUR VANGUARD/INDEX SIMULATED MODEL PORTFOLIOS

Vanguard Portfolio	Total Stock Market Index	Total International Stock Index	Total Bond Market Index
20/80 (percent)	14	6	80
40/60 (percent)	28	12	60
60/40 (percent)	42	18	40
80/20 (percent)	56	24	20

Raw data to produce performance numbers:

Vanguard Total Stock Market Index	1993–2008: actual fund returns 1976–1992: Wilshire 5000 Index − .25% per year 1970–1975: [(0.85*S&P 500 + 0.15*CRSP Small Company Index) − .25% per year]
Vanguard Total International Stock Index	1997–2008: actual fund returns 1970–1996: MSCI EAFE Index − .35% per year
Vanguard Total Bond Index	1987–2008: actual fund returns 1976–1986: Lehman Brothers Aggregate Bond Index − .32% per year 1970–1975: CRSP Intermediate Term Government Bond Index − .32% per year

RISK AND RETURN SUMMARY OF
FOUR FIDELITY/INDEX SIMULATED MODEL PORTFOLIOS

Statistic	Portfolio			
	20/80: Low Risk	40/60: Medium-Low Risk	60/40: Medium-High Risk	80/20: High Risk
Average annual return (percent)	8.64	9.10	9.42	9.60
Annualized standard deviation (percent)	6.99	8.91	11.70	14.88
Worst single calendar year (percent)	−4.68	−13.13	−21.57	−30.01
Worst two calendar years (percent)	−0.53	−10.44	−19.86	−28.77
Worst three calendar years (percent)	7.85	−0.50	−14.82	−27.71

CURRENT COMPOSITION OF
FOUR FIDELITY/INDEX SIMULATED MODEL PORTFOLIOS

Fidelity Portfolio	Spartan Total Market Index	Spartan International Index	U.S. Bond Index
20/80 (percent)	14	6	80
40/60 (percent)	28	12	60
60/40 (percent)	42	18	40
80/20 (percent)	56	24	20

Raw data to produce performance numbers:

Fidelity Spartan Total Market Index
1998–2008: actual fund returns
1976–1997: Wilshire 5000 Index − .25% per year
1970–1975: [(.06*S&P 500 + .15*CRSP Small Company Index) − .25% per year]

Fidelity Spartan Inernational Index
1998–2008: actual fund returns
1970–1997: MSCI EAFE Index − .35% per year

Fidelity U.S. Bond Index
1991–2008: actual fund returns
1976–1990: Lehman Brothers Aggregate Bond Index − .32% per year
1970–1975: CRSP Intermediate Term Government Bond Index − .32% per year

RISK AND RETURN SUMMARY OF
FOUR T. ROWE PRICE/INDEX SIMULATED MODEL PORTFOLIOS

Statistic	Portfolio			
	20/80: Low Risk	40/60: Medium-Low Risk	60/40: Medium-High Risk	80/20: High Risk
Average annual return (percent)	8.54	8.98	9.29	9.46
Annualized standard deviation (percent)	6.94	8.85	11.64	14.82
Worst single calendar year (percent)	−3.40	−12.25	−21.09	−29.94
Worst two calendar years (percent)	−0.55	−10.53	−20.00	−28.97
Worst three calendar years (percent)	7.81	−1.28	−15.15	−27.66

CURRENT COMPOSITION OF
FOUR T. ROWE PRICE/INDEX SIMULATED MODEL PORTFOLIOS

T. Rowe Price Portfolio	Total Equity Market Index	International Equity Index	U.S. Bond Index
20/80 (percent)	14	6	80
40/60 (percent)	28	12	60
60/40 (percent)	42	18	40
80/20 (percent)	56	24	20

Raw data to produce performance numbers:

T. Rowe Price Total Equity Market Index	1999–2008: actual fund returns 1976–1998: Wilshire 5000 Index − .40% per year 1970–1975: [(0.85*S&P 500 + .15*CRSP Small Company Index) − .40% per year]
T. Rowe Price International Equity Index	2001–2008: actual fund returns 1970–2000: MSCI EAFE Index − .50% per year
T. Rowe Price U.S. Bond Index	2001–2008: actual fund returns 1976–2000: Lehman Brothers Aggregate Bond Index − .30% per year 1970–1975: CRSP Intermediate Term Government Bond Index − .30% per year

Acknowledgments

This is my fourth book, and it never gets any easier. Without the assistance of many talented people, it would be an impossible task.

I benefited greatly from the insights of John Duff at Perigee Books.

My literary agent, Carol Mann, of the Carol Mann Agency in New York City, is a continuing source of inspiration and support.

This is the second book I have written with the assistance of Lynn O'Shaughnessy, an extremely talented financial journalist and author.

Whitney Joiner, an excellent journalist, edited the entire manuscript and improved it greatly.

Kent Skrivan, a trusts and estates attorney in Naples, Florida, provided expert assistance with the estate planning chapters.

Sean Kelly, of Kelly & Associates, LLC, West Palm Beach, Florida, reviewed the manuscript and made many insightful suggestions.

Edward S. O'Neal, PhD, a securities expert with Securities Litigation and Consulting Group in Fairfax, Virginia, updated the Asset Allocation Questionnaire, which is the critical first step for all investors to follow.

Henry Hebeler was kind enough to review and provide his expertise on the Social Security chapters.

My Word expert, Nidhi Jain, expertly reformatted many drafts of the manuscript.

Authors routinely pay homage to their long-suffering wives. In my case, Patricia Solin demonstrated once again her great skill as an editor and her unending patience with the process . . . and the author.

Publisher's Note

This publication contains the opinions and ideas of its author. It is intended to provide helpful and informative material on the subject matter covered. It is sold with the understanding that the author and publisher are not engaged in rendering professional services in the book. If the reader requires personal assistance or advice, a competent professional should be consulted.

The author and publisher specifically disclaim any responsibility for any liability, loss, or risk, personal or otherwise, which is incurred as a consequence, directly or indirectly, of the use and application of any of the contents of this book.

Trademarks: All terms mentioned in this book that are known to be or are suspected of being trademarks or service marks have been appropriately capitalized. Perigee Books cannot attest to the accuracy of this information. Use of a term in this book should not be regarded as affecting the validity of any trademark or service mark.

Legal disclaimer: This book provides general information that is intended, but not guaranteed, to be correct and up-to-date. The information is not presented as a source of tax or legal advice. You should not rely on statements or representations made within the book or by any externally referenced sources. If you need tax or legal advice upon which you intend to rely in the course of your business or legal affairs, consult a competent, independent accountant or attorney.

Index

Page numbers in **bold** indicate tables.

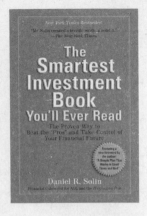
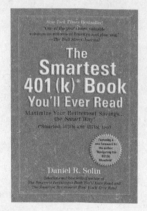

T102.0410